MW00568273

BREAKING THE
SILENCE

OUR STORIES OF HEALING & HOPE

Geoff Brown
Colin Folk
Ramona Iida
Darren Neuberger
Richy Roy, Kelley Wilson

PRESTIGE BOOK PUBLISHING

THIS IS A GOURAMI BOOK
BY PRESTIGE BOOK PUBLISHING

ISBN: 978-0-9959024-5-9
Printed by CreateSpace
Published October 27, 2017
First Edition

Table of Contents

Introduction

The goal of the book is to break down the walls of silence that surrounds people affected by various mental health issues. Too many people suffer on a daily basis (one in five people) and more work needs to be done to provide care to those who need it. But first, people must speak out about it. It needs to be known that there is a serious mental health epidemic happening, and only a fundamental social change can make that happen.

We are starting to see progress with campaigns such as **It Gets Brighter**, **Bell Let's Talk** and **Project ;**, but even more needs to be done than just creating hashtags and retweets. It's a start, but simple semicolon tattoos alone won't cut it (I'm proud to say I've got one on my right wrist). That is why I've agreed to take on this project and do my part to build awareness of Canada's most dangerous hidden problem.

I, myself, have struggled with depression and have witnessed how destructive it is. To tell my story would perhaps be therapeutic as well as beneficial for this project, but I will digress from my original plan and reduce it to an introduction for the time being. Deciding what to write in the introduction is challenging enough. Such a broad and important topic cannot be taken lightly. What better place to look for inspiration then my own home town.

Weyburn, SK, Canada seems to hold an exorbitantly rich amount of talent, athleticism, and entrepreneurship for a population of a mere 10,000 people including the creator of Canada's health care system, NDP politician Tommy Douglas. But the most interesting gem that Weyburn can boast about is the now deconstructed Souris Valley Mental Health hospital.

Built in 1920, and opened in 1921, the Souris Valley Mental Health Hospital was originally known as one of the largest buildings in the British Empire. This building was the birth child of psychologist Humphry Osmond and Canadian architect Kyo Izumi.

Dr. Osmond could be every single Hollywood "mad scientist" character if you were to look at his accomplishments and vast array of trials and experiments including electroshock therapy, hydrotherapy, lobotomies, and for the first time anywhere in the world testing the effects of LSD (mescaline).

"Osmond is best known for his research into the treatment of schizophrenia, and on the other hand the facilitation of mystical experiences, with psychedelic drugs,[1] but his Weyburn hospital became a design research lab to examine the functional aspects of architecture and its impact on the mentally ill. Osmond based his ideas of hospital design on the species-habitat work of German zoologist Heini Hediger, and on the research acid trips he took with Izumi. Osmond also coined the terms "sociopetal" and "sociofugal"[2] to describe seating arrangement that encouraged or discouraged social interaction. His 1957 article "Function as the Basis of Psychiatric Ward Design"[3] is considered a minor classic."

- *https://en.wikipedia.org/wiki/Socio-architecture*

Dr. Osmond was close friends with famous writer Aldous Huxley (*Brave New World*) and introduced LSD to Huxley. Aldous wrote "To make this trivial world sublime, take half a gram of phanerothyme." Dr. Osmond countered: "To fathom Hell or soar angelic, just take a pinch of psychedelic." [the term psychedelic is in fact credited to Dr. Osmond]. After Aldous Huxley took Osmond's advice, he experimented with LSD and later penned the non-fiction book The Doors of Perception, which is what inspired Jim Morrison to create their band's name "The Doors".

At it's peak, the Souris Valley Mental Health hospital housed 2,500 patients and many more workers. It was a self-sufficient institution that had all the employees help with the farming of the land (they grew and ate their own food), maintain the building and dormitories, and even attend mandatory dances held in the grand auditorium.

Regardless of its questionably dark past, it still represents the desire to improve mental health care for the greater good of humanity. What better way to continue that tradition then by sharing our own experiences to help abolish the stigma of mental illness. Building a supportive culture and breaking down these barriers won't happen overnight, but we can start by sharing our stories others.

I want to personally thank all the contributors who submitted their stories for this book. You are champions in the arena of mental health and true warriors at heart.

Richy Roy
Owner & Publisher
Prestige Book Publishing

Forward

CMHA Saskatchewan Division applauds the courage of individuals who come forward with their stories in order to break the stigma around mental illness. Over the last few years, we have seen the conversation grow across the country and people are feeling more confident in asking for help. However, now that we have opened up the conversation, we need to work to make sure that the supports they need are in place. There is still a challenge in finding appropriate, affordable and accessible services.

Now is the time to move from conversation to action. Now is the time to make sure government knows that there is a real need and it is time mental health received the same attention as physical health. We are fortunate to live in a time when the needle is really moving on mental health. Awareness is greater than ever before. Now we have to keep the momentum going and make real change happen. As we all recognize, there is no health without mental health.

Phyllis O'Connor

Executive Director
Canadian Mental Health Association Inc.
Saskatchewan Division

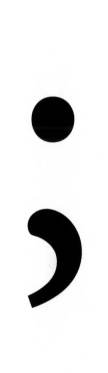

A Cry For Help

I HAVE STRUGGLED to write this story for a long time, for the simple fact that talking about one's own mental health is difficult, but even more so when you are a mental health professional. In the end, it was for this very reason I decided my story needs to be told. People need to know and understand that everyone at some point in time struggles with mental health. If they don't, they probably just don't recognize it. Depression, anxiety, and suicidal thoughts are almost commonplace in today's society and are nothing to be ashamed of. Times are hard, not hard like in the '30s, but hard in a day and age where relationships are strained because people are so busy making the almighty dollar that they don't know their neighbours and sometimes even their own spouses or children. While the '30s were hard, people had the support of their communities and their churches. Nowadays, communities can be made up of people from many countries and walks of life who don't know each other, and churches are frantically trying to entice people in the doors at the expense of relationship and support inside those doors. Not to mention, governments who feel the wealthy should be given breaks while the poor suffer with little to no resources. I was lucky, I had the help when I needed it, and for this reason, I am here to tell you my story.

Looking back, I realize I have struggled with depression since I was a pre-teen. My diaries don't look much different than most teens' would nowadays. Bullying, lack of confidence, not feeling like I fit in, and the list goes on. Many nights and days were spent in tears or just sitting and feeling sorry for myself. These were my private times, the times when I let my guard down and allowed myself to feel. But most times I put on my mask of this tough young girl who would not let anyone affect her. This mask is still on my shelf today.

One of my earliest memories of intense sadness was in elementary school during the numerous times we kids got to make cards or gifts for our dads at Christmas and on Father's Day. You see, I didn't have a dad. Mine had run off when I was two weeks old and rejected me in person again when I was about twelve. My mask told people it didn't hurt when I sat at my desk with my bottle of glue and containers of glitter and made a card for my grandpa instead of my dad, but it did. What was wrong with me? Why didn't he love me? This was a time when single parenting was not as readily accepted as it is now. Don't get me wrong, I have an amazing mom who did a great job raising over one hundred foster kids and me, but the hole of an absent father figure was always there.

Body image was also a big thing for me. As a preteen, I was told I was fat by someone I was very close to; someone too young to even realize how her words affected me, but they did. The roller coaster of dieting started at the age of twelve and continues to this day. When I look back at pictures from that time I am shocked to see that I was completely normal and could only wish to be that fat again lol. It's amazing how as a young person we tend to let others dictate whether we are acceptable or not. Many times during those years I would isolate myself and wish I were not there. I would not say I had suicidal thoughts, but I definitely did not want to be in my situation. I became a doormat. I would often agree to things that I did not even want to do. I let others talk me out of my lifelong dream of becoming a social worker and into becoming an EMT instead. I was scared to death most of the time. Why would people want to put their lives into my completely incapable hands? But each time the phone rang I did what needed to be done for the people in need: I lived a lie for ten years. In hindsight, I think I believed if I saved enough lives I would like myself more and others would like me too. It didn't work. I still felt fake.

Over the next several years, I worked in many areas of the workforce including: justice, retail, labour and human services work. I also married the first man that asked me because I didn't think anyone else would. He was an amazing man and father, but again I felt like a fake. I did not love him like he loved me and I knew he deserved better. I realized he was more of a best friend than a soul mate, but he gave me three beautiful daughters that I could not love more. And I loved him too. He was a good man.

Over the years, I suffered from many bouts of depression. I was in a marriage and job that did not fulfill me. At one point, I was in a workplace that was so abusive and negative that I finally started medication for depression. I was in a hole that I could not get out of. I needed help. But I was tough. I could do it myself and I struggled on.

On March 17th, 2003 came my worst battle yet. I was at work when I received the call from my daughter that her dad was on the floor and EMS was there tending to him.

When I got home I found my husband in the hands of the EMTS I had worked with many times. He was dead. I knew it and they knew it, but we played the game of hope. And we lost. I had lost the one person who was my biggest cheerleader in life, and I had to live with the guilt of knowing that I had not loved him like a real wife should have. Everything started to pile up.

In the next few months, I went into survival mode. I quit the job that I hated and the guilt piled up more as I realized that without my husband's death I would still be there. With him gone, I had the means to start new. And start new I did. I decided to use my husband's "death money" to start a family run restaurant so that I could be around my children all day. As the main wage earner in my family for several years when my husband was alive, I had missed out on many of the important things in my kids' lives. More guilt. But building my dream meant I had to put my trust in a man I had known for many years. I did not have a lot of trust for anyone in those days, especially men because of what had happened with my dad years ago. But I decided to go with my heart and his gentle urgings of "trust me Sandy; trust me." Within months, my dreams were shattered. I had sunk nearly all of my husband's "death money" into our families dream only to find out that I had been duped. The business was not going to make it because the promises made by this man were all false. Even after being nominated for an award for our outstanding restaurant we were forced to close when he chose to sue us, and we lost everything. More guilt as I had lost most of the money that my kids could have used for their education.

Over the next five years, I fought the lawsuit with the help of one dishonest lawyer, who stole from us, and another who helped me from the sidelines to fight the fight of my life. I persisted and eventually won, but it made no difference, as this deviant man had no money "available" for me to win. More guilt and sadness.

About three years after losing my spouse, I was still trying to be the tough one and ease the loss for my kids. I chose to do this by trying to give them whatever it was that would make them happy. It got to the point that they became numb to the gifts and presents and failed to even notice how hard I was trying to make the pain stay away. Instead my own pain was increasing. That Christmas, after spending a ridiculous amount of money buying every gift imaginable and receiving little recognition from my kids, I went outside to shovel my driveway. It was then, through tears that settled into icicles on my cheeks, that I said to myself "I know now why people commit suicide".

This thought, in itself, was staggering to me, and a real

wakeup moment. I realized at that moment that things had gone too far, and I needed help. I decided to call Mental Health that week. It took all the courage I could muster to make that call, but I did. What I didn't know was that the answer wasn't that simple. When I asked to see someone for help the woman on the other end of the line stated, "I can see you in six weeks." Was she kidding? Did she really think I had fought this long and finally given in only to be told the help would arrive in six weeks? I sarcastically asked, "what if I told you I was going to slit my wrists?" To which she replied, "well are you?" I told her that I was not but was looking for some help. In the end, that help came exactly six weeks later.

Starting counseling was the smartest thing I ever did. I was able to bare my soul and share information that I had not felt safe to share with anyone I knew. She was that safe place. She helped me to recognize the distorted ways in which I was thinking and how to work against those distortions. I'm not going to lie and say I was cured immediately, because I was a pretty big mess. I would take two steps forward and one step back. I even went on to become suicidal at one point.

April 1, 2007 was the worst mental health day in my life. I had spent the day before "crying out" for help to the people around me. I sent a note to my counselor asking for help, asked a woman at church for help, and even my best friend. No one seemed to want to answer that call. What I didn't realize was that my cries were not coming in the form of words but in my demeanor and actions. I could not understand how those people could not hear me. Didn't they know that my tears were my voice? That my dead eyes and sad face were my voice? It was the closest I could come to expressing my deep darkness out loud.

On that Sunday, I sat on the grandstand stairs for hours thinking of absolutely nothing but drowning in the deep sadness in my heart. I "awoke" to find the sun going down and the need to feel nature under my feet. I rode my bike over to the Souris Valley grounds and walked the paths crying and sobbing. Why was I so alone? Why did no one care? What difference did it make if I were here or not?

I rode back home in the dusk and got into my car. I had made the decision. I would go out onto a country road, find an approach and drive my car full speed into it. This way no one would know that it wasn't an accident. My kids would not have to live with the shame of a mother who committed suicide. I stopped at the cemetery where my husband was buried and started to say my goodbyes. I was sorry I had not been a good wife, a good mother, a good enough child for a dad to love. I was done. As I started to get into my car I remembered the phone number my counselor had given to me the last time I had seen her. She must have known how close I was to disaster. In that one moment of clarity, I decided to call them to give someone one last chance to show me they cared. I dialed the number and the line rang and rang with no answer. "Seriously?" Even the people who were supposed to help me didn't care? I hung up the phone. Despair closed in around me. The curtain on the stage of life was so far down that I could barely see any light at all. Something in my head told me to try one more time. I don't know why I did, but I did.

The woman on the other line answered on the first ring. "How can I help you?" I paused and stated, "I don't want to be here anymore." She asked where I was and I immediately became paranoid. If I stayed on the line they would find me. I didn't want them to find me so I hung up.

As I started to drive away to my final destination more guilt started gnawing at my brain. That poor woman. If I kill myself tonight she is going to feel guilty. Even in my intense despair I was worried that someone would be hurt by my actions. I was still trying to please people. I decided I would call back to let her know it was not her fault, this would satisfy my guilt. I pulled over and made the call. The woman answered the call immediately. I won't bore you with the details but she managed to talk to me long enough that I had run out of time to take my life. I had to pick up my daughter from her friends at eight pm. I assured the woman I would be safe and hung up the phone. Immediately, the phone sprang to life with an incoming call. My best friend was on the other line. "What are you doing? She asked. "Come to the Dairy Queen for coffee." I sighed and told her I would be there after I picked up my daughter. I knew that this was not the end of my attempts to end my life, but I would have to wait for another time.

Over the course of the next three years, I saw my counselor and worked through most of the issues I had. She was a big help and to this day I am thankful. I went on to finish university and become the social worker I had dreamed of becoming so many years ago. The ironic part is, the first job I took as a social worker was in mental health. Even though I had no idea this was an area I would excel in, I decided to give it a try until something better came up. It turns out this was my calling, the place where I needed to be.

Working in the area of mental health has been a blessing for me. Did it cure my depressive disorder? No, but it gave me a chance to help others who are struggling. Every experience I had went through in my forty plus years became a valuable resource when talking to people about their own mental health. Abandonment-check, bullying-check, self-esteem-check, assertiveness-check, bereavement-check, and the list goes on. Rarely a day goes by that someone does not say how nice it is to talk to someone who "gets it". You see I have chosen to use my pain to help others. It's clear to me that God guided me through every situation so that I would have the experience and knowledge to help others, to fulfill the dream I had of becoming a social worker way back then. Do I ever get depressed? You bet. Do I know how to get myself healthy again? You bet. All I have to do is remember the tools I got years ago and put them into action. And I know too that if I ever need that professional help again, I won't hesitate to ask for it nor will I be embarrassed. After all, mental health is as important as physical health. It's just not given the respect it deserves. Hopefully that changes when people start to come out of the darkness and share their stories so others know that it is ok to ask for help. We all need it at some point in our lives.

Sandy Spencer Johnson

Faith Saved My Life

I THANK GOD for the faith of my Grandmother! She passed her faith to her family, including my mother, who thankfully passed it to her family including me. As a child, I somehow gratefully accepted that gift of faith and made it a part of my life. I remember prayers, rosaries, going to Mass on Sundays and feeling like I had a firm foundation to stand on and something to trust in.

I was married at the ripe old age of nineteen! We had a miscarriage about a year and a half later. That whole experience of a pregnancy I hadn't really planned, learning to accept and be grateful for it, and then losing our baby, was quite a lot to absorb and try to make sense of. Then we moved to my husband's family farm, which was "his" home, but really didn't feel like mine for a long time! He was busy farming, which was always what he wanted to do. It was definitely not my dream, but it had become our way of life, and it was hard work! Over the next five years, we had three sons. I learned that motherhood, although a precious gift is also not as easy as it looked! Because of the combination of these things, I felt isolated, alone, and overwhelmed and questioned my faith! Life was just NOT what I'd expected it to be!!!

I am the oldest of seven children, so my mom was still busy raising my younger siblings. I didn't want to bother or worry her about the depression I was beginning to feel. I didn't have a good friend to talk to and didn't feel like I could talk to my husband about it! More accurately, I believe that a bigger reason I didn't talk about it was because I felt so guilty and ashamed for feeling the way I did. I remember looking up information concerning mental health, but never followed through.

I don't know exactly when the depression started. It was a gradual thing. "Postpartum Depression" was not really talked about then. I also can't remember how long it lasted, but at the time it felt like forever and that it would never end! I cried a lot and was always impatient and angry with my family. My husband likely thought that it was *always* "that time of the month." He had no idea how much I was suffering inside!

I honestly believed that life was not worth living and that, IF there was a God, he was just plain cruel! I really, though totally irrationally, believed that I was all alone and that nobody cared if I lived or died, and I seriously started thinking about suicide! I am horrified to say, that I also thought... that if life was this awful, there was no reason why my children should have to endure it! I actually came up with a plan that I felt would end my life and theirs! I thought about that plan a lot!

As I mentioned before, I had always believed in God, but at this point my faith was *almost*, but *not* totally, non-existent! I continued to go to Sunday Mass and go through the motions, but still about the only faith I had left was what made me hesitate in carrying out my horrific plan! That bit of faith told me that *if* God did exist, then likely hell did also! If I did what I was wanting to do, I would certainly go to hell, and it would probably be even worse there than it was here in this world! (My faith has grown enough now to know that only God, in His mercy, can judge the condition of someone's soul and motives behind their actions, so I certainly don't believe that everyone who has taken a life will go to hell!!)

During this time, we were milking cows and shipping milk. One morning after the milking was done, Harvey was in the house with the kids and I was in the "milk house" cleaning up the milking machines and things. As was a common occurrence, I was crying. I started crying so hard that I had to stop what I was doing. I stood sobbing in the doorway looking across the yard feeling totally helpless, hopeless and trapped and probably even praying to the God I wasn't sure existed! As I stood there, a huge butterfly flew past me into the room. It was so unusual that it definitely caught my attention. It was much bigger than the usual butterflies we saw. It flew right over to where I had been working and crying only moments before and perched on the wall there. I stood and watched it for some time, and it just sat there. I honestly don't know how, but somehow in the midst of my misery, I felt like God was sending me a message of hope, telling me that if I would just hang on, that things would get better. Only many years later, did I find out that butterflies are a symbol of new life and resurrection! I must emphasize that my life did NOT magically become perfect or that my depression completely dissolved, but I did have enough hope to hang on, and I really don't believe that I ever seriously considered suicide (and worse!) as an option again.

My life has changed so much since those years, and it is so full of blessings, I can't even begin to count them. They include another son, three wonderful daughters-in-law, and four amazing grandchildren. It took *many* years till I ever told anyone this story because I think I was afraid what people would think as I sometimes believed it was all just a coincidence, and that I'd imagined something meaningful out of something so ordinary. Besides, telling anyone about the awful things I'd considered doing and why was not an easy thing to do either.

Since then, although very slowly, my faith has grown immensely. I truly consider it to be the most *precious* gift of my life! Now I *know* for sure that God really *does* come to us in the ordinary things that happen in our lives, and we just have to have our eyes open enough to recognize Him! Over the years, I've heard myself saying, "I don't know where I'd be without my faith." But if I think honestly about it, I believe there is a very real possibility that if it wasn't for the foundation of faith that my mother and grandmother gave to me as a child, my sons, grandchildren and I would not be here. I also can't imagine the pain and suffering that my husband, parents, siblings and others would have endured!!!

As I'm sure you must understand, this isn't an easy story to share, but I really believe that God wants me to share my story with others. To be totally honest, it doesn't matter if you don't believe that God sent a butterfly to me with a message! What matters is that you really think... about what a difference the gift of faith could make in the lives of others around you! You all listen to the news, and we hear about the increase in the number of suicides just in our own communities! It does not seem like just a coincidence to me that this is coming at a time when most people are forgetting about God and not going to church. Many people are losing that firm foundation to stand on and are therefore losing hope!

Please, do whatever you can to nurture your faith and to pass that precious gift to those around you, especially your family! After all, it is the only real gift you can give them that can literally last FOREVER!!!

Janice Seitz

Your Valuable Life

MY PERSONAL JOURNEY involves other people's struggles as well as my own…

My childhood memories are happy ones, and I am blessed to have grown up in a loving and caring home. That doesn't mean life was perfect! No one has a perfect life. My parents did all they could for the four of us kids and loved us unconditionally. My brother has his own story in this book, so you can read about his journey. When a loved one struggles, it affects you. Mental illness was not talked about in our home, nor did my parents, nor did any of us know anything about it before my brother's diagnosis. This made it difficult to have respect for what my brother was dealing with during his younger years on a daily basis and challenged some of our family relationships. Looking back, I can see that if we all were better educated about mental illness and had a diagnosis earlier, we could have avoided many conflicts that occurred. But in those days, there seemed to be no help. I am sure it is not easy, but through prayer and knowing Jesus, exercising, medication, counseling, and support from family and friends, my brother has worked hard and finds strength to get through his days.

I have lost some family members to suicide and have others that have attempted suicide. When I was in grade eight, I lost a cousin to suicide. Someone said they thought he was being selfish, but I never saw it that way. I always felt sorry for him and thought how lost he must have felt to take his life. This happened after he broke up with his fiancé. He was a popular young man, handsome and athletic. It shocked everyone. It destroyed his parent's relationship and their lives were never the same. Again, great sadness and loss that shouldn't have happened and should have been avoided. I never thought then that two years later I would be contemplating the same end to my life as my cousin.

When I was in high school something happened to me while dating a guy whom I trusted. I never thought I needed to explain myself more than saying, "No, I don't wanna do that!" Besides that, the way I held my body tight and resisted him should have been enough. I said no and to stop many times. But, I guess for him it didn't matter. The shame I felt after this incidence was beyond what I could handle. I didn't know what to do and was so embarrassed to tell anyone. I started to blame myself as I thought I should have kicked and screamed and fought harder, but I just went numb and couldn't believe the guy I trusted would do this to me. I didn't think anyone would believe me and I felt there was no one I could trust to tell. I thought it would just cause me more problems if people found out. I was so ashamed that I didn't want to be alive anymore. I wrote a note and hid it under my bed saying goodbye to everyone. I wasn't sure when, but I decided to do what my cousin did, start the car in the garage and "fall asleep." I couldn't live with the thought of what happened and just felt "dirty." I struggled for many weeks with this and prayed and prayed. Obviously taking someone else's life was wrong, and I could never imagine doing that to someone else. God revealed to me that my life was just as valuable as anyone else's. I tore up the letter and threw it away. It wasn't easy, but I decided to move on and try to forget about the whole thing. I know now that 'moving on' and not really dealing with this kind of hurt only causes more problems over time. It gets stuffed way down inside you, but still finds its way to the surface over and over in life until you face the pain, face the shame, face the demons... and forgive. This incident had a negative impact on my future relationships and on how I thought of men, as it was difficult to trust again. It was many years later after my husband and I had our son that I finally healed from this incident, when God taught me how to really forgive those who hurt me. (More on that later in my story!) I am now passionate about teaching infant massage, which is all about positive touch, respect and bonding with your child. I am a certified instructor with the International Association of Infant Massage. Parents read their infants cues and understand and respect a 'no' or 'yes' response. This helps the child grow up knowing how to communicate their feelings towards 'touch.' This then promotes other positive relationships in the home, and then, is taken into the world community. I am now exploring taking a course to bring this into the classroom at schools.

I am happy and blessed to be a mom. I looked forward to the whole birthing process and had all kinds of plans to do everything natural when our son was born. I was in Japan at this time. But, there was a sudden change of plans and to spare all details, I had an emergency C-section due to toxemia. I could have gone into a coma before and after the birth of our son, and we both could have died. Then one week later, another emergency surgery in which I needed blood transfusions from losing most of my blood and could have died again. A huge blood clot was removed from my abdomen. I was in the hospital 3 weeks. The difficulties didn't end when we got home. Let's just say I was still healing from two traumatic surgeries and getting no sleep, as well as having multiple nursing issues. I was in a foreign country and just wanted things to be 'normal,' but everything was done differently there. I felt so alone and developed postpartum depression. I didn't even know I had it at first. No one talked about these things. There was no help for someone suffering from postpartum depression there. All I could think of every day was, "I want to run away!!" I knew it was wrong to think that way, but I couldn't help myself. I was exhausted from all the physical and emotional trauma. I didn't want to hurt anyone, but just wanted to put our son down and run out that door. I didn't know if I could ever come back once I left. But, God intervened and did something amazing.

Every afternoon when I started having those thoughts to run away, God took my memory back to a guy I once dated who told me about his own mother running away from him and his family when he was a child, never to return. While dating, he said to me, "If my own mother did that, any woman can, so I have never been able to trust a woman since." This stuck with me and it stopped me from running out that door every day. You see, that guy never trusted women, and in my opinion, it ruined his relationships with them and the way he thought about women. I couldn't stand the thought that if I ran away I would be destroying the chance for my son to have good relationships with women, just like this guy I dated. I didn't want to hurt my child nor destroy his image of women. So, I stayed. But, it wasn't until God taught me how to deal with my past hurts through true forgiveness that these "running away thoughts" finally left me, and I was healed from this depression. It didn't happen quickly, but over the next months, I learned to "Let go and Let God" as I went through steps of forgiveness. It is amazing how God can use past hurts and turn them into a blessing. Now I can clearly see how this man's inability to love and to be loved turned into a message of God's love for me. I am thankful for the lesson God taught me so I would not leave my family. God takes the crap and makes it into something precious! He can do that for all of us. We just have to believe, keep the faith, trust Him and ask. Because I did this, I have a family. I am a mom. I am blessed!!

I needed to forgive this guy who walked out on our relationship years earlier just as his mom did to him when he was a child, without a word or anything. I needed to forgive myself for thinking I was a "bad mom" and realized that this was a lie Satan put in my head. I needed to ask God for forgiveness for judging other moms who actually left their kids or harmed them while being mentally ill, something I never understood before it happened to me. It is amazing what hormones, trauma and lack of sleep does to the brain! I am not making excuses, but until you have been there, you cannot understand it. We do not know what other people are going through and cannot judge other people's choices, even when it hurts others. It doesn't make it ok, but it is not for me to judge. I learned my job is to keep forgiving and love like Jesus. I was finally able to find forgiveness towards others from my past.

Forgiveness does not mean the offense is ok, but it means you admit what the offense was and how it hurt you, and it means that you put the person/people off your hook and onto God's. We don't need to be strong when we ask God to be strong for us. He can heal us and deal with the situation. We then are free to live life without judging this person, without them owing us anything and without living in the lies of guilt, shame or ill judgment of ourselves. Forgiveness equals Freedom! There are actual steps to take to do this, and if anyone wants, I can share them with you. It isn't easy, but without forgiveness, we will be held back and miss out on better things that God has planned for our lives. It will eat away at us inside and keep coming back to the surface to destroy parts of our life and relationships. It is a necessary step in healing and recovery. I deserved that freedom and my relationships deserve that. This has brought great healing and freedom to my life.

Though I have learned about forgiveness, I didn't say it was always easy! Not too long ago while working with some people I found myself being bullied and harassed. I have since had to practice forgiveness again! It went on for so long that it slowly was bringing me down further and further into a deep dark hole. I felt like darkness surrounded me. I didn't want to even try to get out of it for a while and started to feel like no one would really care if I just stayed there. I started to believe the lies in my head, that if I didn't even exist, people would be better off. I really felt like I was in a hole and could not see a light at the top. I was physically, emotionally and spiritually weak. I felt I couldn't move from that black bottomless pit. I believe that we are made in body, mind and spirit, and the health of one of these directly impacts the health of the other two. You cannot separate this. I didn't know where to start to get myself healthy again, but being in this black pit was affecting my relationships with my family members, and I didn't want to keep bringing them down. So I decided to start getting my diet on track (thinking this was the easiest place to start). I know that our nutrition feeds our physical body but also affects our mind. Everything needs balance!

I eventually went to a naturopath to get focused on what my body specifically needed, and at the end of the appointment, she showed me a scan of my body that showed colors representing my aura around me. Everything I had been feeling was right there staring back at me. It showed a thick black cloud swirling around my body up to my head and in the very far distance, almost unnoticeable, was a rainbow of colors. I couldn't believe how accurate this was: an exact visual of what my body, mind and spirit were going through. She said that this black cloud was related to my liver being unhealthy and that liver health is related to anger. Through the whole appointment she kept remarking how bad my liver was and that it was screaming loudly and was not ok! That day, I started to make changes to try to climb up from that pit and see the light again, to start speaking the truth and listening to the truth and not the lies. Again, I needed to find freedom in forgiveness. It took several weeks of eating well, supplements, exercise, infrared sauna sessions, acupuncture, massage, prayer and meditating. I slowly gained strength back in all parts of my health. I literally was looking up from this hole and would try to climb out, sometimes falling back down, and then trying again. I would listen to music that seemed to encourage me to not give up. Songs such as, "Overcomer" by Mandisa, "Gold" by Britt Nicole, "He is With Us" by Love and the Outcome, "He Knows My

Name" by Fancesca Battistelli and many others. Eventually, I started to feel a light shining down on me and felt hope. I felt that hope was God telling me not to give up and that He had better plans for me to come. I felt my situation paralleled Joseph being thrown into the well, and then after some time, he made it to a higher position, one of respect and authority. He was taken from the 'pit to the palace.' I felt I came out of the pit and was now walking upright stronger in God's grace and peace. There is no better place (palace) to be living in than His. One of my favorite verses is, "I can do ALL things through Christ who gives me strength" Philippians 4:13. I needed to meditate on this verse. It was about four months of this before I came out of that darkness and was able to face these people who were treating me this way. When I went back to the naturopath, it was amazing not to see any black swirling around me at the end of that session, and instead, a rainbow of colors and light were circling around my body. I am grateful to so many who helped me heal during those months, and those who were praying for me. Thank you! God answered!

The reason Geoff, Darren and I decided to get people's stories and publish them is because we are all tired of people dying and suffering from mental illness and addictions. We all are affected by this at some point in our lives, just as we all have or know someone struggling with physical health issues. We are passionate to make a difference and this is just a small step we hope will lead to bigger ones in making the difference of breaking the silence, giving hope and encouraging others to keep sharing and keep looking for resources that bring healing and cures to this area of our health and well-being. NO ONE is an island. Do not feel alone, because I promise you there are people going through similar circumstances and there are people who can help support you. Joy and depression cannot reside in the same place. Happiness will come when we learn to love our life no matter what gets thrown at us. Let our faith be bigger than our fears. Love others, love yourself, and love your life. We all have one mind, one body, one soul, and one life to live… let's make it a good one!

Ramona Iida

Suicide Talk Is Not Taboo

MY HUSBAND and I moved to Weyburn from southeast Manitoba in July of 2012, to come work in the oilfield. All was great. The community was very friendly and welcoming. Within days of moving to Weyburn, I got a job at Boston Pizza as a server and my husband got a job in the oilfield. Things were great, we had fun, we were happy, we were saving money, and then in August, the struggle of my life began.

I wish that I had stories to read like this one to be able to realize the signs and symptoms because once I was told what was wrong with me and I received a diagnosis, my symptoms split in half. I'll get to that later. In August, I started to notice that I was yawning a lot when I was not tired, then I was short of breath and had to gasp for air like I had just ran up ten flights of stairs. Along followed heart palpitations, I've had them before, but maybe for five seconds twice a year. This was different. This was almost constant, all day, all night. I felt like I was having a heart attack or that my heart was going to beat out of my chest (keep in mind that at this time I didn't know what heart palpitations were or how common they are). I made an appointment with a doctor and she told me I was just too stressed and to not work so much. Ok, like that was going to happen. I kept moving and doing my thing. A few weeks after that, I started getting heartburn and acid reflux all day, every day, also having no idea what it was because I had never had even mild heartburn before. I went back to the doctor and she prescribed me Tecta, a daily pill to lower acid in your stomach that I ended up taking for a year to no avail. Within that year, it got so bad that I couldn't eat much more than soup and water because the acid erosion made my esophagus incredibly sensitive and feel like food would get stuck. I lost twenty pounds and only weighed eighty pounds. I could not afford to lose weight because I am already only one hundred pounds eating normal.

With all those physical symptoms came some pretty scary mental and emotional symptoms. My first time in the Weyburn emergency room was... two in the morning and I woke up my poor husband who had to work the next day to take me. I couldn't breathe, I was hyperventilating for no reason, and at the time, I thought

I was dying. We get there and they did some tests and told me I was having a panic attack. Well then, now what? I didn't think those could come out of nowhere about nothing. That was one of many panic attacks, but again, once I knew what it was, it made me less scared and I could handle it. From then on, it only got worse. I cried all the time for no reason. I was terrified of everything. I couldn't go to the grocery store without fear of everyone starring at me. I would be driving down the highway going 80km/hr, white knuckles on the steering wheel in plus thirty-degree weather, worried that I was going to roll my car. All my fears were irrational and I knew that, but that didn't make them any less real at the time.

After about a year of going to a doctor who made me feel even more like a crazy person, I switched to a doctor who was able to see the bigger picture and within 15 minutes of meeting with him, he told me he thought I had an anxiety disorder and depression. From there offered me some counseling and treatment options. What a relief! *Take note: if you feel your doctor just isn't cutting it, SWITCH!* Had I continued to go to that other doctor, who knows where I would be right now (probably going for a CAT scan because I would be worried about having a brain tumor because of a headache or something). I was irrational, but it felt real.

Suicide. I know, a taboo subject, but it can't be! Tell someone! Tell as many people as you need to. These thoughts are not uncommon even though no one talks about it. You would be surprised. I am proud to say that I have never attempted, but it has been a thought that has crossed my mind from time to time. It takes a lot of courage to tell someone, but once you do, you won't regret it.

What helped me?

I saw a counselor, I was medicated, and I had a great support system. Coming to terms with the fact that I needed treatment to function did not upset me. Some people need medication for diabetes and some people need medication for high blood pressure. I just needed medication for a mental illness. I'm no different than anyone else and I can live a full and amazing life with this.

I saw a good doctor who makes sure that I am well taken care of.

My husband is my world! I don't know what I would do without him! Through everything he has stuck by my side, made sure I am well taken care of, made me feel as normal as possible and doesn't pressure me into doing things I'm not up for. For example, if there is a get together that our friends are having and I just don't feel up for it, he suggests cuddling on the couch and watching a movie instead. He is just too perfect.

My parents are wonderful. From their generation, it isn't the norm for things like this to happen to people, and it wasn't something people talked about in their day, but they have given me all of their undivided attention when I need to talk and they are so open to trying to understand. It is unreal. They have so much love to give. I know a lot of people that don't have a close relationship with their parents, and I am so grateful I do.

My brothers are awesome at making me feel normal. Typical tough loving big brothers, they don't treat me like anything is wrong or that I'm different in any way. I am still their same little sister. It makes me feel good that they don't baby me in fear of upsetting me. I love them to death!

I have too many animals! Can you have too many? I recently adopted a dog from the humane society and I love how much of a mummy's suck he is. I love feeling needed! I love the bedtime cuddles and the good morning face wash an hour before my alarm goes off. I love how excited he is to see me when I get home!

My friends. They are just so understanding, and I have so much fun with them that it almost makes me forget about my mental illness.

The happy ending to my story...

In all this time, I have made sure to make my place in the world. I married my wonderful husband in June of 2016. I have traveled by myself to Toronto and flew on a plane to take a permanent makeup course, something I had to challenge myself to do. I own my own successful permanent makeup salon in Weyburn, and I love what I do. My job is stress free, almost relaxing, and I make people feel beautiful!

My advice...

You CAN get through anything. You CAN do anything you want to do. DON'T be afraid of failure! Keep your goals HIGH! Push yourself to do things you normally wouldn't do! Don't be afraid to ask for help! There ARE others like you! You are NOT alone! Don't give up!

My name is Harmony Melnychuk and my story isn't over yet.

Harmony Melnychuk

Stolen Joy, Stolen Time

WHEN I MADE the decision to put my story down on paper, it didn't seem that difficult. However as I sat down to actually complete the task, it felt like I was gearing up to climb Mount Everest. Where do I start? What do I include? Will people judge me? Will my children read this someday and what will they think? Ultimately, it's these questions that push me to do this. People need to know. They need to know how bad it can get, and they need to know that there is a way through. I take comfort in the thought that perhaps there was a purpose to my excruciating battle with depression. Perhaps part of the reason I had to go through so much pain and darkness was so I could share my story and give hope to those battling it now and those that may deal with it in the future. I need to do this for the families and support networks of those people, including my own children.

Now I find myself sitting on my couch, the computer in front of me trying to summon the will and the energy to organize my thoughts. And it all takes me back to the journey. Days upon days of sitting on the couch and trying to summon the will and the energy to begin what should have been the simplest tasks: getting up and doing a load of laundry, washing dishes, making a meal. Even going for a walk was too much. The twisted thoughts in my brain could keep me stuck in place for hours. It would start with this inability, but the sadness would follow, as I would beat myself up for not being 'normal.' The day I sat at my kitchen table while my dad cooked a pizza from my freezer, brought my kids home from daycare and fed them, the only thought in my head was "why can't I?" Why couldn't I get the pizza from my own freezer and cook it? Why couldn't I pick up my kids? Why couldn't I feed them? Why couldn't I do something so simple?

The answers are never simple and straightforward, and sometimes the search for answers would lead me to beat myself up more. I have a great life with supportive family and friends. I couldn't ask for anything more from life. I felt I had no right to be depressed. Yet, there I was. Glued to the couch. The constant thoughts running through my head would eventually lead to my lowest point involving a brief stint in House 10, the local psychiatric unit, right before Christmas.

I have a family history of depression, perhaps it's hereditary. I have battled bouts of depression in the past; maybe I'm just a little more imbalanced than some. Without question the trigger for this latest episode was hormones. I had experienced post-partum depression before, but a quick prescription from my doctor and it was all under control. I managed to struggle through after the birth of my third baby but slowly fell into the pit of depression. I clawed my way through day after day, just trying to keep my head above water. I thought I could do it alone. And then I went back to work. The added pressure and stress was the final straw, and I collapsed. The demons had won the battle; they would not win the war.

I was fortunate enough to be facing these demons in a country where healthcare is a right. I was also fortunate enough to have amazing people on my side to pull me back up when I was knocked down and to walk with me, support me and often carry me through this journey. After many medication trials I finally found a combination that worked well enough for me to function. Between the medications and lots of counseling, I was better, but my psychiatrist recognized that I wasn't as good as I could be. He referred me for Transcranial Magnet Stimulation. These treatments involve a series of short magnetic pulses directed to a small area of the brain to stimulate nerve cells. This has been found to be effective for treatment-resistant major depression but is still not a widely known option. The treatments themselves were quick, but I had to drive an hour each way, every day, for eight weeks to complete the full course. I wasn't that good yet, so my pizza-cooking, kid-feeding dad drove me every day and my always dependable, drop-everything-to-help mom took on the kids until my husband would get home from work. It was worth it.

After the first week of treatments, my husband and our oldest boy had a hockey tournament to go to. It would be fine; I had slowly improved with meds to the point that I could look after the younger two alone for a day. But something had changed. One week of treatments and I had the best day I had for years. I enjoyed my kids. My little guy was three years old, and I broke down at the end of the day because for the first time in his short little life I had enjoyed him. I always loved my kids, I would have done anything for them, but I would also tell you how trying they could be. Suddenly, I not only loved them, I liked them, and I wanted to spend more time with them. I was crushed that depression had stolen that time of joy from me but so excited to now have that feeling back.

Every week of treatment revealed more things I had been missing. Suddenly everything was clear – it was like the difference between snowy black and white reception on TV and watching high definition format. I had forgotten how beautiful the color of the sky is; it's my favorite shade of blue. One week, I suddenly realized that I have a beautiful flowerbed in front of my house. I always knew it was there and always spent lots of time working in it, but it suddenly had flowers in colors that could take my breath away. I was alive. For the first time in years, I was completely alive.

I don't have all the answers; I still ask the same questions sometimes. But perhaps this book will help me answer the 'why.' I needed to be open and honest and share, in the hope that someone else may benefit from my pain. I hope it helps.

Amber Istace

Resources that helped me:
TMS with Dr. Natarajan - Acupuncture with Taka
Win the Battle: The 3-Step Lifesaving Formula to Conquer Depression and Bipolar Disorder; Bob Olson; Chandler House Press; 1999
The Noonday Demon: An Atlas of Depression; Andrew Solomon; Scribner; 2001
Depression, the secret we share; Andrew Solomon TED talk

Solace In My Misery

MY STRUGGLES with depression, anxiety, and identity began right around the time I turned twenty-five. I grew up in the electronic age where everyone's thoughts, dreams, nightmares and personal lives were thrown on the Internet for anyone to see. It was a way for us, as youth, to feel immortal, even if things turned up not so good as a result.

Looking back at my life, when I turned twenty-five, I realized how silly and inadequate those things were. It also made me ashamed of myself. I would see old photos or posts on Facebook and scream inside at the teenage boy spewing my emotional carnage over the Internet. I was curating my life to fulfill the needs of others. It made me feel really disconnected with myself entirely. I felt as though I had been wearing a mask to please others, or acted a certain way because that's what was expected of me. It also made me, and so many others, prime targets for cyber bullying.

For two years, until I turned twenty-seven, these things haunted me. The thought of not knowing who you really are or that you were a self-made pawn for people to play with, mixed with the fact that this was a petty and juvenile issue, sent me down a negative path. I became distant with family and friends. I didn't open up about my true feelings, in fear of judgment. I stopped eating, sleeping. I lost more weight than I could afford to lose and became very sick. No one could see that I was actually hurting inside. As a result I perpetuated the issue that was taunting me. I couldn't face myself let alone anyone else. I was constantly depressed, but hid it. I was frustrated with anxiety, but never spoke about it.

The odd thing about this two-year journey was that I was subconsciously creating my escape. Being a photographer for several years allowed me to interact with so many different people. In my head was this endless supply of creative fuel. Without knowing it I had found solace in my misery. It was a beautiful thing to feel! All this depression and anxiety is strong, but I can be stronger. Why not use that raw emotion for something that could not only help me, but also possibly speak to others? It became the inspiration behind my second solo photography exhibit "Becoming Human."

Featuring a very close friend as the subject matter, the eighteen-piece exhibit showcased my transition from something heavy into something lifted. Realizing that the past shapes us on purpose, we are always evolving, and changing. We are who we are for a reason. This taught me that we have to accept ourselves first and not let others dictate our lives. Society doesn't control our futures, we do.

Chris Borshowa

Why Aren't You Happy?

I HAVE STRUGGLED with mental illness for close to 30 years. I don't really know what my problem was, but I certainly wasn't crazy---like to need a shrink, I just wasn't happy, no big deal... Well actually it is a big deal. Life is meant to be lived happy and well.

If I knew then what I know now...

This is an exercise I did not too long ago. A little letter I wrote to my younger self:

My sweet young Dawna. I get what you are feeling. I get what you are going through. I get that you believe your aches and pains are real and you "feel" sad. I get that there is nobody to talk to. You certainly do not want anybody to think you are crazy. You do not want to go away for help. You do not want to have to take pills. You do not want to be different than your friends, so you hide; you hide who you are and what you feel. You play the sick card, not feeling good card, nobody can argue with that. Who can argue with not feeling good? My sweet Dawna, you need help. You are not well in your heart. Let me help you. Let me tell you. Let me show you. You can be free to be who you are. You do not have to be the person others think you should be. Stop living for them. Your belief about "doing whatever it takes to make others happy then you will be happy" is not true, and it will not work. I can help you. I understand you. I get you. I will not judge you. I will not tell you that you are wrong. You have so many people that love you and will support you. You have to talk. You have to tell your story. Live through this fear and speak your truth and what is inside. Be free and move through this. Where there is will, there is a way. God sent you to this world to be love and to give love. The dark, sad days are not what God had in mind for you. He planted a seed in each of us, and He is with us, waiting to watch us grow into beautiful flowers in His garden. Take my hand. We will get through this. We will get through this, and then we will help this world smile and love and embrace every day and every opportunity and every obstacle together. We got this.

Love me.

I struggled in my teenage years with unhappiness. And the frustrating part of it all was I had no reason to be unhappy. I had a good family, good friends, good grades, was athletic, etc., etc., but I wasn't happy. Why wasn't I happy? I couldn't tell ya. So I decided that once I grew up, graduated and was on my own, then I would be happy. I headed out into the grown up world and still felt sad. I ended up moving back to my hometown, got married to the greatest man in the world and started a family. Everything should be good now, but it wasn't. What is my problem? Again the question: why in the world are you not happy? You have everything: a wonderful husband, beautiful kids, you don't have to work outside the home, you have lots of close family and friends, you have this and you have that. So Frustrating! What was my problem?

I accepted that I needed "help" as my days and ways didn't only affect me anymore. I had a family to take care of. I guess it would come down to counseling and antidepressants.

I am thankful for the love and guidance (and prescriptions) I received from my two amazing doctors, but I will forever be grateful to have been introduced to a special lady in mental health. She taught me some amazing strategies to acknowledge and accept and move with or through some of the issues and "thinking" I faced. She also encouraged me to Google up and check out a program called "Everyday Living" with Joyce Meyer. One day something Joyce said instantly triggered that I had better days to come but I had to make the decision to choose better days! I grew up with God in my heart, and now Joyce was reminding me to keep God first. He is the "Peace" in my puzzle for living my greatest life. I knew, I totally knew, I would be going off the antidepressants (with the help of my doctors who supported my decision). The Rx never really worked for me. The side effects were significant, and we were forever increasing doses or changing or adding another pill. I hated being numb. I felt like I lived in a fog. I am truly blessed to be able to manage my mental illness without prescriptions any more.

In today's world (and with the internet) there are so many wonderful people and services that can help with mental illness. I am not saying that medical doctors and prescriptions are not needed in some cases, but there are so many other options out there that can help you get to the root cause of what is troubling you. There is a reason for everything, and we need to get to the center of it, and then work through it. But you have to be willing to be real and true and get to the BS (call it bull shit or a belief system) that we live with. I learned that one of my greatest BS was guilt by comparing myself to others. We need to live for ourselves. Stop comparing. Every person in this world is on his or her own journey, and we need to focus on and live for our own. Who are you when you wake up each morning? Don't let somebody else decide what your good enough looks like. Do what you need to do to live your life with passion. Don't start your day with the broken pieces of yesterday. Every day is a fresh start. Each day is a new beginning. Every morning we wake up is the first day of our new life.

Again, I used to think that if I could "help" everybody be happy, I would be happy, but I have changed that way of thinking and have learned that if I am happy and take time for myself, then I am much better for all. With the Internet and Facebook and Twitter and so many great authors and transformational coaches out there, there is no need to give any of your focus, time or energy to negative or bitter people and information. I look to inspirational and motivating people that find the good in every day and every situation, good or bad... what you think about and read about, and listen to and watch day after day, is what you manifest and bring into your life. Let it be something good!!

I am blessed that I have a wonderful doctor who is willing to work with my amazing naturopath. In the end, we are all working towards the same result: living well with an amazing energy and happy health. I also see an amazing body talk practitioner and transformational coach: Amy Dawns, and I love her to death and all that she has brought to life in me. I have participated in a number of sessions of Neuroptimal brain training at Neurofitness in Regina, which are super good! Proper nutrition, exercise, yoga, journaling, music, dance, fresh air and sunshine are a must for me as well.

I am not ashamed of my struggles. I am who I am. It's all Good.

Dawna Mellon

The Silent Epidemic

MY NAME IS Pamela Guest, and I suffer from mental illness. I am here to get my message out there to millions of others that may be suffering from mental illness in silence and not to just end one stigma, but also to shatter two stigmas.

I want to speak to you about an unimaginable act of stolen innocence and emerging flight from the shadows of darkness, to shatter the stigma of mental illness due to another silent epidemic that needs to be brought to light, which is sexual abuse, one of many causes of mental illness.

I have PTSD, major depression, insomnia, anxiety and

panic attacks due to a silent epidemic that our society lives with across this world. In my teenage years, I struggled with all that I just mentioned but also with shame, guilt, fear and thoughts of suicide. If you looked at my childhood, it was picture perfect, but there were secrets that I was keeping as a young child, secrets that no child should be keeping, and it's a secret that so many children around this world are keeping and staying silent about today.

Did I have the words to tell someone what was happening to me? No, as I had not been educated on how to speak up and tell, so I kept it a secret for twenty-four years.

It wasn't until the spring of 2010, at the age of twenty-eight, that things in my life were being drastically affected from the trauma of the sexual abuse. I spiraled into a deep depression and hit rock bottom in which I started going to see a psychologist. In April 2010, I broke my silence. I was meeting one on one with a psychologist, once a week for the first six months, then every two weeks for the next six months, and once a month for the next four years, and once every two months for the next two years. To this day, I still have appointments if I feel the need, so that I can continue to heal. Going to see a psychologist has helped me deal with the nightmares and flashbacks, which are all signs of PTSD (Post Traumatic Stress Disorder). It has also taught me breathing techniques for the anxiety and grounding techniques, so when the PTSD is happening, I know how to get back in the present and not continue in the past of the trauma from the abuse. The stigma for mental illness and sexual abuse survivors is huge. So much shame to talk about these dirty things that happened behind closed doors. I can remember that moment as if it was just like yesterday, as this kind of trauma lasts a lifetime. By the summer of 2010, I was prescribed an anti- depressant, anti-anxiety and sleeping pills for the next four years to help cope from the trauma of the abuse.

Throughout this time of seeing a psychologist to get help, I was suffering from some migraines, and on June 23, 2011, I was having a hard time functioning and concentrating. I started getting numbness and tingling sensations, shaking uncontrollably throughout my body and then went paralyzed on my left side of my body. I had a droopy face, speech and hearing impairment. I called 911 and was rushed by ambulance to the my local hospital where they did all kinds of medical tests (CT Scan, M.R.I., EEG, TEE and tons of blood work to determine what was happening to me. At first, they thought it was a stroke, then meningitis, then a brain aneurysm, then blood clot due to the birth control pill, and at that time, they were ruling it out as hemiplegic migraines. I was put on a strong medication for migraines, released after a week of being in the hospital and just told to monitor my health.

In January 2012, I had a second episode with all the same symptoms as the first episode. I was hospitalized again, for a second time, for a week with the same medical tests completed six months prior in which they also added a brain wave test and spinal tap to rule out the possibility of other health conditions. This was the second time that all the test results were coming back negative saying they cannot find anything medically wrong with me. It was at this time that my neurologist asked me if I had been under any stress lately or had been through any kind of traumatic event in my life. I then disclosed to him that I was sexually abused as a child and have been receiving treatment by a psychologist for the past 10 months. My neurologist came back the next morning stating that what was happening to me could be an underlying of a type of mental illness of what is called conversion disorder (trauma manifested in the body that comes out in physical symptoms or ways with no medical cause) due to the trauma of the sexual abuse and staying silent in which it may take time to fully diagnose.

In March 2012, I had my third episode, and then a month later, I had my fourth episode, in which I was starting to recognize the signs and symptoms and just handled it on my own the best I could. When having these episodes, they can last from twenty-four hours to seven days with the use of a wheel chair, walker and then a cane (I would like to note that I did not have any of these episodes until after breaking my silence). Silence makes you sick.

In May of 2012, I was admitted into the psychiatric ward overnight at my local hospital due to suicide. By the end of this month, I started a cognitive behavior therapy called E.M.D.R. (Eye Movement Desensitization Reprocessing) also what they use for War Veterans to treat PTSD. Within a year and half of doing E.M.D.R., it was the fall of 2013 when I had a last flashback, from the sexual abuse, and woke up at 4:10am. I believe I was given a second chance by the grace of God. God was sending me a message that morning. "As each has received a gift, use it to serve one another as good stewards of God's varied grace" (Peter 4:10) This was God's way of telling me my purpose, and why I need to stay here on earth. It was at this moment that I realized that this was a gift to finally come out of my cocoon and emerge into a beautiful vibrant free butterfly spreading my wings and flying beyond horizons, being the change I wish to see in the world.

"The purpose of life is to discover your gift. The meaning of life is to give your gift away." It was shortly after that I read "Unimaginable Act" by Erin Merryn and was inspired to stand united as survivors in determination to give victims a voice. This was the moment that I chose whether to be silent or to stand up about this epidemic that is happening in our world today. My voice has grown louder. Weakness, fear and hopelessness died. Strength, power and courage were born.

By the end of October 2014, I had a fifth episode. It was at this time that I had been seeing a psychiatrist for over a month, and it was determined that in the past four and half years of not knowing what was going on with my health, that I do in fact have conversion disorder due to being sexually abused as a child and staying silent.

I am sharing my story so that others do not feel alone. That it is ok to break your silence and to reach out to get help for mental illness. By laying the foundation in my healing by reclaiming my voice, I would not be here today, proudly telling you my struggles and achievements of this unimaginable act, if it had not been for breaking my silence and getting the treatment for mental illness from psychologists and a psychiatrist over the last seven years making me realize the abuse was not my fault. I have nothing to be ashamed of and helping me work through the stages of my life of how this is affecting me of being a wife and mother.

Why don't we wake up this society to these silent epidemics? We live in a world where we look the other way and pretend it's not going when it's going on in all of our own backyards. Every single one of you knows someone that is going through a mental illness or this has happened to, you just might know his or her name. Let's turn something tragic into something positive by making a good change out of it.

The journey of my purpose had begun from late October 2014 to the present. This purpose was to stand united with Erin Merryn, the co-founder of Erin's Law, as she has inspired me to help her to get her law to go international.

Since October 2015, I have been pursuing Erin's Law in my province of Saskatchewan for it to go international. Erin's Law will provide an age appropriate curriculum for children, youth and school personnel on sexual abuse starting from Pre-K through grade twelve. It aims to educate children, youth and school personnel on unsafe touch, safe touch, unsafe secrets, safe secrets, how to get away and tell if someone is sexually abusing them or being photographed inappropriately and that the perpetrators are held accountable for their actions. Erin Merryn, the co-founder of Erin's law, is a two-time survivor of sexual abuse and has passed her law in thirty states. Erin's mission is to pass the law in all fifty states in the Unites States, and then go international by passing her law throughout Canada.

Throughout 2015 and 2016, I have had many meetings with MLA'S, Saskatchewan Advocate of Child and Youth Bob Pringle, Ministry of Education Don Morgan, and sent a letter to Premier of Saskatchewan Brad Wall, as well as had countless meetings with Executive Director of the Ministry of Education of Saskatchewan Curriculum Unit. I also have a petition that has been introduced into Saskatchewan's Legislation in support of a sexual abuse prevention curriculum for the province of Saskatchewan to take immediate concrete action to develop and implement Erin's Law. Such legislation would ensure that a comprehensive health education program be developed and implemented, which would require age-appropriate sexual abuse and assault awareness and prevention education in grades Pre-K through 12 along with training school staff on the prevention of sexual abuse.

In October 2016, nearly one year after starting this journey of testifying Erin's Law for the province of Saskatchewan, I had a fourth meeting with the Ministry of Education of Saskatchewan Curriculum Unit Executive Director and was delivered wonderful news that the Ministry of Education of Saskatchewan were taking immediate concrete action to develop and are implementing a Child Abuse Prevention Education and Response program from Pre- K to Grade 12 that would include Sexual Abuse Awareness for children, youth and school personnel for the province of Saskatchewan. I was given an invitation to take part in a meeting that would take place to have input in the development and implementation of a policy statement that would outline a sexual abuse prevention education. I attended the meeting in person at the Ministry of Education of Saskatchewan Curriculum Unit and there were 46 organizations that took part in this meeting and 16 them were school divisions.

To date (Oct. 2017), I am currently waiting for the Ministry of Education of Saskatchewan Curriculum Unit for the next step to be taken for the sexual abuse prevention education in Saskatchewan's Education Curriculum starting in the fall of 2017 being taught to all schools in the province of Saskatchewan.

Since Erin Merryn has passed her law in thirty states, in the past five years, school presentations have been made in the states that have passed Erin's Law and children have disclosed to teachers, school counselors and trusted adults. In all of these cases, the perpetrators were held accountable for their actions.

I am grateful and pleased that the Provincial Government of Saskatchewan acknowledges that changes needed to be made in the education curriculum, however my mission was to pursue Erin's Law, for it to go international, and that is *not* being administered. My next step is that I am currently still working to have a brand new bill developed for the province of Saskatchewan, Canada that would be introduced into Saskatchewan's legislation that pertains to Erin's Law that would be addressed in 2017 speaker session for the final conclusion to my mission of not just implementing a Child Abuse Prevention Education and Response that is currently being developed.

I would like the Provincial Government of Saskatchewan to not just agree to the current changes that are being made to the education curriculum at this time, but to implement it as "Erin's Law," so that children get their rights met, understanding that they will be believed, along with it being reported to authorities to ensure that their perpetrators will be held accountable for their actions and that by having a "law" known as "Erin's Law" implemented in Saskatchewan would ensure that the education curriculum would not be subject to being altered or become different from its original purpose in the future. As a province and community, it is our shared responsibility to protect children and teach them the skills to keep them safe and to be protected by a law.

I want to shed light on the stigma of mental illness and also shatter the silence of the stigma of sexual abuse. By ending the stigmatization of both of these epidemics in this world, we will be a society that understands that it is ok to talk about it, receive help and give awareness. I also want for anybody that may be going through mental illness or who was a victim of sexual abuse not to be ashamed, to know that there is help out there and to get help. There is light at the end of the tunnel of all this darkness. I have persevered with strength, courage and hope, and you can too. Let's talk to end the stigma of Mental Illness and Sexual Abuse.

Sincerely; a Survivor of Child Sexual Abuse,

Pamela Guest

Erin's Law - http://www.erinslaw.org/erins-law/

Road To Mental Wellness

FOR CONSTABLE Jeff Bartsch, the dusty, endless miles of Saskatchewan grid are his therapy, and his purpose. Jeff is a member of the Weyburn Police Service, and a person who has found his cause.

About ten years ago, Bartsch was a twenty-one year old working as a police officer in a small and isolated community. "I made about two years and my world caved in." Long hours of working alone, with few supports or opportunities to leave the community to recharge, caused a landslide of anxiety and depression, which eventually caused him to quit his career and nearly cost him his new marriage. As his situation reached a crisis, he secretly went to see a psychologist, not wanting anyone at work to know the extent of his struggles; however, they were not as hidden as he had believed. The next day his supervisor presented him with a paper, ordering a mandatory psych test. Jeff notes, "On one hand, I beat him to the punch. But I was stressed. What was this going to mean for my job? Who was going to find out? Who was going to judge me?"

It is unwritten but inherent; police culture does not encourage its members to talk about pain, fear and sadness, but Bartsch admits that he couldn't even talk to his parents about what he was going through. "It was the hardest thing, telling my dad." He was so proud of me and talked about my career all the time. I told him after I had already quit." Real concerns about job security and the perception of other officers equates to mental health issues which become unnecessarily severe; which Bartsch believes could be alleviated or eliminated if only people would start talking openly about it. He does admit, "This was hard for me at first. Everyone was asking why I quit policing and I didn't want to tell anyone what I was going through."

He spent a period of time trying medications to get his anxiety and depression under control with only moderate success and he didn't like how they made him feel. That is when he started to run. "Running leaves you with your thoughts. It teaches you bellying breathing, deep breathing, which reduces your heart rate." Deep breathing is known to reduce symptoms of anxiety and calms the brain, allowing it to think more clearly. And he began to feel better.

After working for a time as a long-haul truck driver, he decided to give policing one more try. "I always knew I wanted to help people and that's what policing is about." With the unwavering support of his wife Ashley, Bartsch enrolled in the Atlantic Police Academy, and it opened up a new world of education about mental health as it relates to both police officers and the people they serve. "I was blown away. Every day for six months, we were taught about mental health. I left believing we should all be talking about this. So when people ask why I left policing or why I would be crazy enough to try it again, I tell them my story."

And that story attracted the attention of some police officers in the U.S., some of whom had their own experiences. One officer Jeff spoke with had been forced into retirement for seeking professional help, a departmental policy that undeniably conceals the rates and severity of mental health issues in that department's members. Jeff's U.S. contacts provided him with the partnerships and support that propelled him toward competing in his third, and most meaningful, marathon. In May 2016, after many hours of specialized training on long stretches of road, he ran the Saskatchewan Marathon in full uniform (yes, including the heat trapping vest) to bring further awareness to mental health. At the time, only four other people, all from the

United States, had ever done this.

Jeff's connections and the social media accounts that documented his journey helped him achieve his goal. Jeff's Twitter account exploded with messages from other police officers who commended his efforts to bring this issue out of the dark, and let him know that they too had been affected. Since his marathon, he's been contacted by individuals across North America who have been inspired to run their own races.

He speaks firmly about his desire to educate people about the difference between mental health and mental illness. A mental illness can look like many things, but "it can often be something that is treatable, but not necessarily curable," says Bartsch. Mental health refers to a person's state of mental wellness, not unlike the wellness of a person's heart, lungs or eyes. He believes many people's issues with depression and anxiety spiral out of control because of the stigma. "When we get a toothache, we go to a dentist. No one is embarrassed of that. But when we have mental pain, we ignore it because we are scared to talk."

During his time at Atlantic Police Academy, he learned some secrets about maintaining mental health. He believes every officer should be mandated to have a mental health checkup. He also believes that all people should perform mental health checkups on themselves. "How am I feeling? Am I withdrawing from loved ones? These are the questions people should ask themselves and then be aware of coping strategies so they can help themselves."

Bartsch admits that the road to mental wellness was a long one but credits his wife Ashley for where he is today. "It nearly cost me my marriage. But I chose her over the job and if she had left, I don't think I'd be here." Jeff was hired on with Weyburn Police Service in October 2015 and says he is glad to be back in his home province. He is also grateful for the good working environment and supportive supervisors, which he didn't have during his first stint in policing.

His goal of increasing awareness has not stopped at his marathon. He is a resource in his place of work, participates in public speaking and training across Canada, and regularly attends a support group at the Weyburn Canadian Mental Health Association, in uniform, where he introduces himself as Jeff. He is passionate about being an advocate and has remained true in his desire to help others. Marlo Pritchard, Chief of Weyburn Police Service, says this about Jeff: "When we interviewed Jeff, he was forthcoming about some of his past struggles. He also came across as honest, sincere and meticulously prepared. He is a great fit for our organization, is passionate about policing and has become a leader in this community. His dedication to mental health awareness is phenomenal. As a society we need to stop talking about mental health and physical health. It's health. Period."

When Jeff is asked if he allows himself some pride in all he's accomplished, he quietly admits he does, then adds, "But I never wanted to be famous. Just if I can help one person."

Jeff Bartsch

Originally published, in part, in Blue Line magazine, March 2017 edition. Written by Lisa Miller

Journey Through Post-Partum

MY JOURNEY OF STRUGGLING with mental health issues started with my second child. I was diagnosed with post-partum depression, four months after she was born. There just seemed to be a heaviness over me that would not leave, and I always felt stressed. I decided it was because I had just had a baby. I had no sleep because my baby hardly slept during the night, and we were extremely busy being pastors in our community. What made it even harder is that I lived in a small community, which I had moved to that year, and now when I look back, I felt very isolated in. I had some support, which I was thankful for, but it still was very hard. My husband was a pastor then, which has its own challenges, that I believed added to my stress. My husband was gone helping others a lot, and I felt very alone most of the time. I had a baby and a toddler, and I didn't have a lot of help, so most of the caregiving was done by me. I remember feeling out of control and overwhelmed almost all the time. I lost a lot of weight because I would forget to eat because I was taking care of my babies and our home. I was a mess, but looking back I thought this was normal. This is what a young, new mom is going to feel like. Little did I know, this is not what I was supposed to feel like at all.

When my second child was eight months old, I found out I was pregnant again. I was not happy at the time because I knew that in my mind and emotions I was not ready to have a baby again or that my body had healed from the last pregnancy. I did go through with the pregnancy though and had another beautiful baby girl. Week by week went by, and I started to feel overwhelmed and full of anxiety again, but this time, it was even stronger than the last time. I literally thought I was going crazy. I remember asking Brandon, my husband "Am I going crazy?" I could not sleep during the nights, which I believed compounded the idea that I was losing my mind. He reassured me that I was not going crazy. I thought I was going crazy because I had emotions that I could not control which scared me so much. I remember cuddling with him so that I could feel his heart beating and that would calm me and hear his breathing, which I would try to fall asleep to because my breathing was not relaxed. Finally after three really difficult days, I decided to go to my doctor and get help. She looked at me and listened to me. Then she said that I needed to be admitted to mental health in Weyburn or stay at the Radville hospital. I decided to stay there, as I was so scared to go to the mental ward. During that night there, I remember hearing voices in my mind saying, "Just end your life" and "you are going crazy." I remember having extremely scary nightmares in which I woke up in cold sweats. I was afraid to be left alone as well. I was put on medication right away, and I was diagnosed with post-partum depression and anxiety. I was so close on the scale of having post-partum psychosis, which is what they rated me on the scale they give when assessing patients. I didn't want to be myself, so my mom came down and watched the kids for over a week while my husband took off a month work to take care of me. I was scared to be around knives, which is not a normal fear either, and I remember I was not left alone for that period of time. The medication I was given made me sleep a lot. I remember that I would sleep two times a day and for long periods of time. It was hard because I felt exhausted so much of the time, but I still tried to be the best mom I could be for my kids. After a while, the medication started to not work for me and I decided to go off of it thinking I don't feel bad anymore. I am better. I can go off of it now. I was not better. Going off of the medication cold turkey made me spiral. I started vomiting and couldn't hold any food down. I went through drug withdrawals, which caused me to almost start the whole process over again (balancing my chemicals in my brain). I was sent to a psychiatrist in Weyburn, who had me try two different antidepressants before the third one worked. This process was very hard because by then, I was watching my kids and my husband was working again, now in the construction field and had very long hours working. I remember struggling again and wondering if I would ever feel good again. I was losing hope that I would ever be me again. I felt like I was gone. I struggled so much with hopelessness and could not see my future. It felt like my life would never be the same. But day by day, month by month, year by year, my life did begin to change. I began to change. I put in the work to get better. I went to counselling, and I began looking after myself. I did the things I needed to do to get better, and I trusted in my God to get me through. I did get through with my faith, my husband, my family, and my friends. It has been a slow process of healing and wholeness.

I still have many days, especially the last year where I've had to process pain over again because the loss of my brother who was traumatically found dead in the valley in Estevan. I have had to learn to feel again, really feel and to learn to choose how I am going to handle the pain. Mentally, I have to learn how to deal with trauma and how to deal with it in a healthy way. I have been going to counselling and that has really been a benefit to me. I could so easily let my depression take over me, as I have a reason to feel depressed. I choose to fight it and not let it take over me. I have to fight it. Some days are really hard (I am not going to lie), and some are easier than others, and it is getting better. I have hope now. Hope is my anchor. I am breaking the silence so that others who have similar journeys, like mine, do not feel alone. That they feel loved even in their pain and suffering. That they can have hope. That they can conquer their depression and even triumph over it. This is my journey.

Angela Tichkowsky

Talk To Your Loved Ones

MY HEART IS FULL of gratitude to be able to share in this great cause. I hope our stories, which you're reading, will touch the lives of someone out there who is possibly struggling with depression, mental illness or perhaps thoughts of suicide. If you are struggling in any way, I just want to tell you that you are not alone, you are valued & important, your family and friends all need you in this life, and most importantly, you are most precious & LOVED. So don't ever forget that because you really are. If you need help, please go to a doctor to get medication that can help.

On a personal note, I too have friends that have left this world early from taking one's life. Did you know that 50% of men and women never seek help or go for treatment before it's too late? It is truly a tragedy because this single act leaves so many victims lost and hurt: first the one who dies, then the other dozens of family and friends who are left behind some to face years of deep pain and confusion. The living victim struggles, often desperately with difficult emotions of guilt, grief, anger and rejection, all of which the victim's family feels. I have seen it so much in the eyes of others as it pierces my soul. I have personally fought a few bouts of depression in my life from going through a divorce, losing family, losing a few failed businesses, all of which rocked my world and turned it upside down. I can relate somehow battling through such a loss as I have sampled the effects it has on a person emotionally and physiologically, and believe me it's not fun. Luckily, I have found a higher power, God, and a purpose to this life to help me through what I call survival mode and the trials and tribulations I have been given and endured. At different times of my life, I have felt His presence and His hand in on it to help me make it through. For which, I am sincerely humbled, blessed and grateful for.

I know we were all put on this earth for a greater purpose: see each other through and we must strive to find that purpose or perhaps contribute to a greater cause like this book. It feels so good when we can help and serve others. I know we are all capable of planting a seed and making a difference and spreading kindness and love to others, which we all need in this life. Maybe you need to heal and love yourself before you can love others. I understand and get it, and I'm here for you. Your friends and family are here for you too. I believe in you and you can make it through this. Once you get through this little hiccup or trial you're experiencing, you will be able to help those that are struggling to find their way again and encourage them to stop seeking out the storms and enjoy more fully the sunlight. As this life is so beautiful and blessings and happiness await them. I know you can do it and believe in you. Here are some signs to look for in others that might be struggling with depression:

1. Loss of interest in things that used to be pleasurable
2. Sleep difficulties
3. Eating changes
4. Anger and irritability
5. Expressing negative thoughts
6. Suicidal ideas
7. Loss of confidence in one's self
8. Loss of optimism about the future

If you see these things happening in yourself or others encourage those loved ones to seek help as you must seek treatment to help you get through this time. I promise you things will get better when you keep going, serve others and stay busy. Sincerely tell them you mean the world to them and reassure them you care and love them so much. Mention, "I don't know what I would do without you. Yes, please don't give up. Always remember there is a way out of this hell, and we'll get through this together." Don't miss these signs as they are crucial, and you don't want to regret that it's just too late. Sometimes, the most powerful tool to help someone is to simply reach out with friendship and words of love and encouragement. As you know in our culture talking about suicide is taboo and is often swept under the rug, but this is very real, and we must someway talk about it, be more understanding & compassionate, and reassure them that we are not going to leave them to suffer alone or abandon them. We must be proactive, but most importantly, seek the medical attention they need.

Maybe you could say to a loved one, that is experiencing this pain, "I'm here for you. What can I do for you right now to help you?" Showing compassion and just being there to listen makes all the difference. What kind of thoughts are you having? It's not your fault. It may not look very good right now, but please remind them that the feelings are temporary, and you'll be right there with them to get through it. Maybe say, "We're not giving up on this... It's you and me against this depression, I will go with you to seek the medical attention you need, and we will win and make it through together." Tomorrow will be better. I promise you.

To conclude, I wanted to share some spiritual comfort from church leaders to those that might have lost a loved one by suicide to give them hope and assurance of a bright future ahead for your loved ones.

Suicide consists in the voluntary and intentional taking of one's own life, particularly where the person involved is accountable and has a sound mind. Persons subject to great stresses of life may lose control of their selves and become mentally clouded to the point that they are no longer accountable for their acts. Such are not to be condemned for taking their own lives. It should also be remembered that judgment is the Lord's; he knows the thoughts, intents, and abilities of men; and he in his infinite wisdom will make all things right in due course. And it is requisite with the justice of God that men should be judged according to their works; and if their works were good in this life, and the desires of their hearts were good, that they should also, at the last day, be restored unto that which is good.

I believe the Lord will consider each case separately and judge the circumstances of each individual. I have sincerely sought direction from our Father in Heaven to help me understand the nature of suicide. I have come to know, as well as anything else that I know from God, that these people have a place in the kingdom of our Father, and it is not one of darkness or despair, but one where they can receive much comfort and experience serenity.

As I think about the worry and agony of those whose loved one has taken his or her own life, I find deep comfort and faith in the Lord's promise and blessing to us who remain in mortality: "Peace I leave with you, my peace I give unto you: not as the world giveth, give I unto you. Let not your heart be troubled, neither let it be afraid."

Just remember - be optimistic. Faith can overcome fear.

It isn't as bad as you sometimes think it is.
It all works out.
Don't worry. ...
The Lord will not forsake us.
He will not forsake us.
If we will put our trust in Him,
if we will pray to Him,
if we will live worthy of His blessings,
He will hear our prayers.

Geoff Brown

Trigger Point

I GREGORY JOSEPH BROWN, was given a diagnosis of paranoid schizophrenia when I was twenty-nine years old. My life seemed to have been quite normal up until that time. It was at this time that I experienced the tragedy of our son dying at birth. Doctors have told me that this shock triggered the onset of my mental illness. At that time, I was fully employed and was enjoying life with my dear wife, Bonnie. A terrible twist came to my life, as things just seemed to spin out of control.

I sought medical advice and was hospitalized for six months in a row, off and on, over the years. I was given the last known medication and therapy. Over a period of a few years, my wife and I had two beautiful daughters.

A few times I went off my medications because I thought I could go on with life without them. During these times it grew difficult to hold a job. These and other factors, like not being accepted by others, led to the break-up of my marriage and separation from my daughters. My life then took on a completely different kind of darkness. If not for the light and the peace I found in Christ, my life would have continued on in darkness.

Now, I have found the strength to go get the medication and needles that are necessary for a person with my disability. I know that this has to be a top priority in my daily life. It is as necessary as keeping in touch with my Lord Jesus and the fellowship I find in my church family. I am also very blessed to have had a mother, father, brother and sisters to stand by me.

My message to others who are experiencing mental illness is that there is light at the end of the tunnel. Seek help from professionals, follow their advice and find strength in God.

Greg Brown

Insidious Illness

WHERE DOES ONE BEGIN? When my sister approached me and asked me to share my thoughts on mental illness, I will be honest I was very hesitant. To begin, I will have to go way back to when I was a young kid growing up on the farm. I was probably around twelve years old or so when I can recall my first major anxiety attack, though I did not know what it was at the time. Back in 1977, no one really knew or talked about mental illness, let alone a twelve-year-old boy. There was only "normal people," or you were "psychotic," or in a mental institution. There was no mental illness, no Prozac, no depression or anxiety.

It was taboo to even mention anything to do with a "mental condition or sickness."

In those days it was called "the blues", or you are "just feeling sorry for yourself."

One of the first memories of my mental illness was once I was sitting in the tractor doing summer fallow in the field, and it could just happen out of nowhere. This terrifying feeling that you were going to die and you felt totally helpless. It could be triggered by anything. Then the panic, fear, sadness, total despair would just wash over me where I could barely breathe or think clearly. It sucked. I would usually cry for hours out in the field, and then feel guilty for some reason, sometimes to the point where I would have to stop the tractor and get out and take a walk to calm down. It hurt, and I wondered if this was normal. I spent a lot of time thinking if any of my friends felt like this? Does everyone have this? I guess this is just the way it is. Little did I know that I would have to deal with this for the rest of my life. Looking back, I guess it was good I didn't know what it was, or it could have overwhelmed me at that young age to know that there's no cure.

Mental illness is insidious. It's silent and persistent. It never takes a day off or eases up.

I learned over the years to hide it. I learned to mask it in many ways. I played sports, was popular, and tried to make people laugh all the time. A class clown I was.

Years later, I would just drink to mask the pain and sadness. That just made it worse, obviously. I was very social and loved being around family and friends. But when that was over and I was alone with my thoughts I would break down.

Usually in my room with the door shut tight in case mom would come in. Being on a farm I could go out to my favorite spot in the garden and just hide. Try to hide from the world. Cry and cry a lot. I would sit out there with my dog Patches and cry. Then go back to the house and put on my fake face to show that I was ok. My parents never knew...

I got to a point where I was going to commit suicide. Yes kill myself.

I couldn't take the pain anymore. Just a deep, dark, black hole with no light at the end. I thought my family would be better off if I was dead. I thought I was a loser, a fake, a horrible person, and the world was better off if Paul was gone.

As the years past, this happened a lot. Frequent would be an understatement. I sometimes don't know how I made it. By the grace of God I think. I battled depression for years before I finally realized that I needed help. With my families support, I did get help. I was diagnosed as chronically depressed and probably since childhood.

Low serotonin I was told. Had no clue what that was at the time. Prozac was prescribed to me. Within weeks, I felt better. Happier, less nervous, more relaxed, safe. I felt like a different person. I could focus, and think straight more. All that from a small pill.

I only wish that I had the medication twenty-five years before. I still battle, but the battles are less frequent, and less intense.

I hope that if anyone reads this, just talk to someone. Anyone. Just do it. Don't suffer in silence as I did for thirty years. There is help. I'm proof of it. Talk and someone will listen.

Don't be silent.
Ask and get help.
Life is way too short.
God bless everyone.

Paul Heebner

More Than Just Baby Blues

It's NO SURPRISE that becoming a mother is a huge life change. Everyone knows that, and we were ready for it. We bought the stuff – the crib, the wrap, the tiny booties and the diapers. I was prepared for the poopy diapers and the constant worrying, and even for the multitude of nighttime needs. What I was unprepared for was losing myself.

I experienced the usual "baby blues" that I was warned about. I remember walking (hobbling to be truthful) through my front door after being released from the hospital, standing in my front entry with a three-day-old baby, a sore body and swollen feet, and bawling my eyes out. It would hit me now and then – that uncontrollable urge to cry, the confusion and forgetfulness. Again, I expected it. I was ready for that.

What I wasn't ready for, was my extremely fussy and hungry baby, and for the overwhelming guilt I felt when I couldn't feed him enough. You see, he was a big newborn. Nine pounds and three ounces. He did some damage coming into the world, and I suffered for it. I was very low on iron and in a lot of pain. Breastfeeding wasn't easy, and he was hungry. Like ridiculously hungry. I did the work. I saw lactation consultants and tried to eat the right foods. I tried to "relax" and just let my miraculous body do what nature intended for it to do (because we all know that is SO easy to do when your world is imploding).

We reached a point where my son's hunger and discomfort (yes, we were also blessed with some pinched nerve difficulties) led him to wake up every hour at night, asking for food that I couldn't give him and looking for comfort. For him, that comfort was sleeping on my chest in a recliner in his room. Not a restful sleep for mama, but anything for my baby, right? Because this is what we do as mothers. Whatever it takes. We give and give and give until there's nothing left. Until we're a fractured shell of the person we were. And we don't even realize it's happening until we are so far gone that we don't recognize ourselves.

You see, that guilt that I felt over not being able to nurse him was the beginning of something much bigger.

Looking back, I can see how detached I felt from everything. How I loved my son but didn't brim with that earth shattering joyful love that I was promised while pregnant. I did fun things with him, danced and talked with him, offered him sensory toys and played peek-a-boo with him, but I don't think I was totally present. It's as if I was doing these things because I was expected to, and not necessarily because I wanted to. It's hard to explain, even now, how I could be happy and sad at the same time.

Part of my struggle was because I wasn't sleeping. None of us were. Our days and nights ran together in a blur of fighting for sleep and naps, and worrying that we weren't doing it right. With that worry came the guilt. The all encompassing "everything is my fault" guilt. The "I should know how to do this!" guilt. I felt bad for everything. I felt bad when I was pinned under a sleeping newborn on the couch and not cleaning the bathroom (which desperately needed it). I felt bad for not having anything prepared or even considered for supper when my husband got home from work. I felt bad for not wanting to shower. I felt bad when I didn't enjoy every magical moment of my new son's life. I felt bad for not being happier.

The truth is, I was depressed. And tired. And falling apart. And putting myself last.

When my son was six months old, we hired SleepWell Baby. I can't even explain how much that helped. Here was this person, telling me that everything was ok, and I wasn't going to irreparably damage my child by teaching him how to sleep somewhere other than on my chest (thanks for the fear tactics, Google & horrible advice forums!!) and that doing something to improve my own quality of life rather than solely focusing on my baby was going to make me a better mother. And it did. Sleep was my ticket to finally healing my body. Sleep changed my fussy baby into a happy drooling baby. Sleep put me back in bed with my husband. It was life changing for us and I can't thank them enough for it. It didn't fix everything though.

When my son was two years old, I broke down during a conversation with my husband. It was while my son was napping, and I recall things getting really out of control for no real reason. Suddenly I was crying over literally nothing. The floodgates opened. I admitted that maybe I wasn't cut out to be a mother because anything this difficult and unnatural feeling surely can't be a right fit. I remember saying, "I'm just not good enough at it." I was still going through the motions and I had what seemed to be the perfect (and most adorable) child and husband, but I was watching my happy moments through the haze of an observer, never fully feeling anything. We decided that I needed help, and I made an appointment with a counselor.

At our first appointment, she asked, "What brings you in today?" and I couldn't even get words out. I just ugly cried and said I didn't exactly know, but I knew that something wasn't right. That I didn't feel like myself. Over the next weeks and months, we worked through what I now know was my Post Partum Depression and I've come out the other side. I'm a better wife and mother, but the most important thing is that I'm me again. I recognize myself. I feel things fully again. I'm present.

I'm not sure how things got so out of control for me. I once mentioned my emotional state to my doctor at a routine visit for my son, and she attributed it to the "baby blues." I didn't press the issue. Don't make waves, right? I put on a brave face for the lactation consultants at our frequent visits. We were always focused on my son and how I could do more for him. Nobody ever seemed to want to know how I was holding up, so I didn't offer. They praised me for being "such a good mom!" and trying to breastfeed for so long. The health nurses weighed and measured him, wanted to know how much he was pooping and peeing, and at the end of the appointment would always ask "And how are you doing?" while they busily wrote their notes down and checked the time. I was an afterthought. And I was ok living in that role. At the time, I don't think I even knew that what I was feeling wasn't "normal." I've never been a mother before. Maybe this is what you're supposed to feel.

It's not.

I think my main obstacle in getting the help I so desperately needed wasn't a lack of support or resources available to me. It was allowing myself to ask for help. You see, I'm the one who helps people. I'm the one who saves the day and fixes the problem. I "have it together." I run a business. I'm an intelligent and talented woman. I'm strong. That didn't fit with what I was feeling and so I kept it hidden. Nobody around me knew I was trying not to drown because I didn't let anyone know. I certainly don't think my husband knew the full weight of my PPD until I broke down that afternoon with him. I let him see it, and everything changed.

I'm better now. I still get emotional when I talk about my "dark days," but it's no longer coming from a place of guilt or shame. I feel some anger now. Anger that I lived for more than two years in a way that wasn't healthy or necessary. Anger that nobody recognized how my deteriorating mental health was affecting my family. Anger that I missed out on that feeling of exploding and all encompassing love for my child for so long. It's there now. I get it. I look at him, and I could burst from it. And it took nearly three years to get here.

This anger that I feel will fade, and this will soon just be something that I went through. I do think it's important to talk about though. This experience will affect my choice to have more children or not. It will also most certainly affect my husband's choice to have more children or not. He's gone through it too, but in a different way. He had a front row seat to my decline. I can't imagine how scary that was, but the fact that we're talking about it changes everything.

So do that. Talk about it. Talk to your friends or your doctor or a counselor or your parents. Put it out there and start getting some help. Because that Earth shattering love is worth it.

Erin Francais

The Answer Is Hope

MAYBE I WAS WRONG, but I always considered myself a very strong person, being able to cope with many situations that came along in life, from having many alcoholic family members to deal with, to caring for a mentally challenged aunt for many years, to coping with way below average farm commodity prices on the farm for a few years plus BSE and figuring out how will we survive and feed our family and having a brother and a cousin commit suicide, to also working off the farm at a high stress job for 20 years.

But, when my son who was 18 at the time, came home and told me he had gotten himself into big time trouble relating to heavy drug and alcohol use and had committed a crime and robbed some people while pointing a pellet gun at them I thought he was joking. No kid of mine could possibly do something this crazy. Not knowing whether to believe him or if this was a fabrication in his mind from using hard drugs I searched his vehicle to see if I could find anything to rationalize what he was telling me was the truth. I found credit cards in two peoples names I did not know, and I found the pellet gun. So it was true, and my heart sank to a place it had never been before.

My son said the police were searching for him, but he wanted to come home and tell us what he had done and that he was sorry.

It was like a story you watch in the movies! I was having a very difficult time absorbing and processing that this was actually happening to my life. Your mind goes from accepting this is true, to how can I fix this, to what is going to happen to him, to this is hopelessness and fear that sets in and is added to this chain of thinking that goes on in your mind. Over and over your thought process goes, and then terrible panic attacks started occurring, causing me to lose sleep for a number of days. When I was able to fall asleep, I would have horrible nightmares and wake up in a sweat. I could think of nothing else. I have never been so scared in my life, nor have I felt so helpless to do anything to rectify the situation.

Within mere days horrible depression, which I was unaware was even happening until I could feel myself becoming totally helpless and physically curled up into a ball and mentally sinking into this black hole, set in. And yes people, it was a black hole! It was very real in my mind! I looked up and could see light, but no matter how I tried to reach the edge of the hole to pull myself out, I just did not have the strength to do it.

I could hear my husband talking to me, telling me that everything would be ok. But I didn't believe him.

At this very moment in my life a friend had heard what had happened and stopped in to see how I was managing. I guess she could see I was not managing at all. And after talking everything over with her, her words to me were, "Your son needs you more now than ever, just to be there for him. You are no good to him if you fall apart. You must pull yourself together and be there for him even though you do not know what you can do to help. I know your son. He is a good kid, but has just made some very bad choices in life. God will see you through this and help you make the right decisions on how to help. There is hope!"

Her words gave me one thing, the hope I know I so

desperately needed! I was able to pull myself back out of that black hole and look at the situation a little more clearly and started figuring out a plan to get through this nightmare.

I did seek help from my doctor at this point.

I know the majority of people will read this and not be able to comprehend what I am saying, and I totally understand. Unless you have gone through this, you do not fully understand how fast your mind can fall to such a low. Now I understand what the last few hours of someone's life is like that contemplates suicide and the mental pain they are going through.

I have heard many people refer to people that commit suicide as being very selfish, not thinking about how this will affect their families and they are taking the easy way out.

In my case, my mind got to a place where I was completely incapable of thinking of anyone else. Your mental pain is so great that it totally consumes you. So unless someone intervenes at this point, as in my case, I was unable to come out of my depression myself.

"Hope, stay strong and God will help you through this," is what got me to come back to reality. My friend saved my life!!

I have never suffered from depression any other time in my life. I have never abused alcohol or drugs. Everything happened so fast with me. It seemed like I had no time to think about asking for help.

I thank God for sending my friend at that exact right moment in my life.

If you see a friend or someone going through a difficult time, be kind and reach out to them. You never know. You could be the hope they need to latch on to.

Carol Borys

I Am Mikayla

Hi I am depression. I am eating you up from inside to out. But I am also anxiety. I am worried about being eaten up.

Hi, I am depression. I am going to make you feel like you do not want to live another day. But I am also anxiety and oh boy, I cannot leave, I have things to do!

Hi, I am depression. I am going to push all your friends away. But wait, do not forget, I am also anxiety, and now I need my friends back by my side. What will I do without them?

Hi, I am depression. I am going to be unloving to your family and say hurtful things. But yes, you already know, I am also anxiety. Wait, please! I did not mean to hurt you guys!

Hi, I am… I am no one. I have no friends; I have hurt my family; I have lost myself, and really there is nothing left of me.

I use to be ashamed of my illness. In fact, it still kind of embarrasses me at times. You know how some days you wake up and it is grey outside but then other days it is sunny? That is how I feel. I woke up yesterday with a sunny mind, but today I woke up to grey clouds. I do not really know why… Why my body feels like I have been stabbed a million times, time and time again. I do not know why yesterday I wanted to succeed, but today I do not feel like living. I do not know why there is constant worry in my mind, worrying about worrying about worrying.

I was diagnosed with depression and anxiety in the seventh grade. It is really a blur, but I remember the doctor telling my mom that I was probably suffering from it. I remember being given my first prescription for antidepressants. I remember visiting my first counselor and being so scared. I remember all those 'stupid' questionnaires the counselor made me fill out asking how I felt when they knew how I felt; for heaven's sake why else would I be here! I cannot count the number of counselors and/or doctors I have seen to this day. Although I do not enjoy going to them, I know that they are there if I need.

When I have an outbreak, it is hard. I have lost many friendships. I have distanced myself from my family, but the worst part is losing me. There is nothing worse than hating yourself because if you do not love you, how can others love you. This, I believe is hard for people to understand. They give us "space" and time for us to come back together not knowing what else to do when in reality we need them there; which is why it is time to stop the stigma on mental health and educate those around us. I know I will deal with depression and anxiety eating at me for the rest of my life. My goal is to not let it control me; I am in control! It will always be a challenge, but I hope the good days far outweigh the bad days!

There is something about telling my personal life to people that I do not like, so I have learned to cope on my own. Some days I cope better than others; some days I have no energy left to fight; but some days I am ready to kick the day's ass. One way I have learned to cope is to workout. I have been power lifting for six years, and honestly, I do not know how I would have made it through some of my toughest years without going the gym. There is no better feeling than hitting the weights, and for that moment, forgetting everything happening in the world around you, and taking all your frustrations out in a sweat. I also have a daughter now, and I know she saved my life. I am young, and I am also a single parent; I hated myself for the longest time for doing this to myself. How could I possibly take care of a child when a lot of the time I cannot manage myself? Somehow all those worries faded after she arrived, and although this is the hardest job I have ever done, it is also the most rewarding. When I feel like I would be better off dead, I look at her and know she is why I am still here. I worry about my daughter having a mental illness, but if she does, she will know I will be here to support her in her brightest moments and her darkest days. Most importantly my family never left me alone in my struggles and I will never leave my daughter alone in her struggles. We are a team and will always be together.

One in five Canadians will experience a mental illness throughout their lifetime. That could be your mother, your father, your co-worker, your neighbor or even you. Regardless of who experiences it, a person should know that it affects us all. Mental illness is an invisible disability, which means that you may not see me suffering, but it does not mean that I am not. One of my high school counselors asked me one time, " how do you get up every day and battle with your mind?" I told her I just do, because if I do not, I have lost to myself. I refuse to let myself lose this battle and I hope you never lose your own either. I am here for you. Let's talk.

Who am I? Mikayla. Mikayla is my name. I AM NOT depression and I AM NOT anxiety.

Mikayla Lohse

Suicide Sucks

I 'VE OFTEN JOKED, "Mental illness doesn't 'run in our family'." It stops, gets to know you, shakes your hand, stays on your couch for three years..." but never stopping to sympathize with the many losses we have encountered.

It's a great mask to hide behind when people around you may feel hurt and uneasy, and I don't want them to hurt... so I make light, and smile, and laugh... but never forget, I also understand that maybe that is exactly what that person needs to hear instead of jumping off the bridge!

I guess I'll never know how many lives of my friends I have touched or have helped them decide to live just one more day?!

One thing I have noticed of my peers that have taken their own lives - they too seemed to care about protecting others they love.

I think if someone were to ask, "How many people here have thought of committing suicide?" And if they didn't put up their hand, I would want to be in that room to call BULLSHIT!!! Healthy or not, it is completely normal to think or imagine what would happen if we were to take our own lives. Not saying I've been close to following through, but I have imagined "which route" would be the easiest or most noble or respected (for lack of better wording).

Obviously (and thankfully) I am a procrastinator, and I have decided I just want to hang around through the good and the bad, to see my final days, and how I meet my maker when he is ready for me! I think all of us feel an obligation to serve God, a higher power, or even just our fellow man or community.

There is no better feeling than knowing that I make people smile and laugh! It's like a drug to me. I think it's very crucial, that we as friends help our struggling friends and neighbours. I appreciate what you guys are doing, and I am truly proud to hear your voices amplify what I have been thinking for many years! "It's okay to feel down and hopeless, and we want to listen!" Really listen! We might not have all the answers, but we do have great direction, and we can help guide you to a safer place and a happier tomorrow where we can see you again!

Oh how I would love to run into Perry out on the lake fishing some day and be able to say to him, "Remember that time you were really feeling down about that problem you told me about? I bet you're sure glad that's all behind you now, eh?" (Man that was hard to type without a tear... impossible actually).

My heart goes out to all the moms, dads, brothers, sisters and the many friends who are suffering every day because of the loss of their loved one. I understand the sorrow and heartache, and I also understand their anger and rage!! It's hard when we don't have an answer because the person is not here to answer the questions!

Though I don't feel there is ever a good way to die, suicide is definitely the worst! Not only are we left with no answers or reasons, we are also burdened with not hearing about the pain that person was going through.... and the unfair guilt we will hold onto that we weren't there to stop it! SUICIDE SUCKS!

I think it's important that this book, "Breaking the Silence," do just that. By sharing stories and "Talking about it." It will give us comfort and hope knowing we are not empty and alone. We share all those rotten feelings that others do, and we are strong enough to endure the rest of the journey! It's not a race... We can take as much time as we want! We can stop and pause when we like, and we will continue to move on, just as those who have left us would find comfort in us going on!

Peace my brothers and sisters. We are family!

Jeff Heisler

Bully Brain

MY NAME IS Tanis Francis, and I have been living with Obsessive Compulsive Disorder (OCD) for as long as I can remember. For me, I have to check things over and over, to make sure that they will not cause harm to others or to myself. I make sure the doors are locked and shut, all of the lights are off, everything is unplugged that could cause a fire, etc. I check, literally, everything. Things you wouldn't even think of!

I have certain "checking routines" that I have to perform in the same order each time I do them. This takes a lot of concentration, as well as silence so I do not lose focus. If someone is talking in the background for example, I have to wait until they are finished speaking so I can finish my routine. Otherwise, I feel like I may have missed something so I have to start checking over and over again.

One of the main obstacles I face, because of my OCD, is that I do not cook. I probably can cook, and have maybe five times in my life, but I worry that the stove or the burners will be left on and the house will burn down. Another compulsion I have is to check that the sink taps are off, every time I wash my hands. Unfortunately, I am also terrified of germs and contracting disease or illness, so I wash my hands A LOT! My hands are always red and have sores on them from washing them so much. Aside from those fears, along with general fears everyone has, I worry that I've ran over somebody every time I drive. Even if I do not see anybody on the road, and trust me, I'm a very alert driver; I worry that I might have hit someone. I realize this is a very unrealistic fear since I pay attention to everything around me, but that doesn't make it any easier in my mind.

Basically for me, having OCD is like having two different brains. One brain is logical and knows that I shut the stove off, unplugged the curling iron or locked the door. But the other brain is a bully and says, "WHAT IF YOU DIDN'T? "The house will burn down and it will be your fault. The sink is on and it will flood the house. What if someone breaks in because you forgot to lock the door?" Unfortunately, I am forced to check everything over and over again until it feels right and safe. However, at any moment, the "bully brain" could come back and put another scary and unrealistic idea in my mind, forcing me to go back and check again.

I have been going to a mental health councilor since I was sixteen, and am on medication from a psychiatrist to help with the OCD. One thing that I've found on my own to help me with my OCD is telling myself that life is too short to stare at a sink tap, for example. When I'm 90 years old, am I going to be happy with the fact that I wasted so much time on illogical thoughts in my mind? No, of course not. I need to keep believing in myself, and I can eventually find a way to beat this OCD. You can as well, with whatever you are dealing with! Stay strong!

Tanis Francis

Emotional Strife

THROUGHOUT MY LIFE, members of my family have been affected by alcoholism, depression, anxiety, drug addiction, mental and physical abuse. Some were just crazy! The mitigating factors (i.e., the drug and alcohol usage of some) escalated the bouts of depression in others. I have had multiple family members attempt suicide multiple times, but only one was successful. Over our lifetime, my family became very disjointed and dysfunctional. It affected some of my siblings more than others, to be sure, but we were all affected.

Unfortunately, growing up in Weyburn, there was very little support for these types of things and few people that could provide any type of aid. Doctors in the '70's and '80's were complacent and just prescribed more drugs without any feedback from mental health experts. We were not allowed to talk about any of the issues as that might embarrass the family and affect the family business. My brothers and I shared our situation with very few close people.

I found that while abuse of any kind will reside with a person for a lifetime, physical wounds heal; but the emotional strife will last a lifetime. I like to call it the herpes of mental health… It never goes away. But it can get better with the right support systems and choosing healthy people with whom to spend your time. Find these people and understand that these types of afflictions are common and the more you can talk to about it, the more comfortable other people are disclosing to you what is happening in their life. It's not easy, but it's essential to know that you are not the only one that has issues, and together you might be able to help each other feel more secure.

Kathy Gagne

Family Matters

MENTAL ILLNESS surrounds each and every one of us. Many of us aren't aware of the signs and symptoms, therefore, do not understand mental illness. It has lots of names... She/he is weird, crazy, dysfunctional, etc. I am 51 years old and mental illness has been a part of most of my 51 years.

My father was an alcoholic and an abusive man. Alcoholism is not listed as a mental illness. I have a different perspective. My father drank to get away from any "feelings" or "reality" he was faced with. He and his siblings were sexually abused by their father as children and, I believe, he couldn't deal with the anger, shame, embarrassment and blame he felt. He drank to run away. He drank to forget. He drank to be funny. He drank to have friends. The problem is... no one can outrun or drink the feelings away. The feelings are always there, waiting for you to deal with them. When the feelings got too close or too hard to deal with, he lashed out and abused my mother, abused his friends, abused his partners and abused his self. He could have had depression, a personality disorder, bi-polar disorder or any number of other mental illnesses with a name. He never went to a doctor and was never diagnosed with any sort of mental illness. His medication of choice was alcohol. He could have chosen to get help, but he didn't. My parents divorced when I was four. We moved away from him. He wasn't involved in our lives, only an occasional visit once or twice a year. He passed away at the age of 51.

My brother, Sheldon, was my only sibling. He played some sports but didn't excel at them. He was a bit of an introvert. He had a few friends. We were close as kids, normal sister/brother fights, but we also had each other's back. When Sheldon was a teenager, he started to experiment with drugs and our relationship became a more distant. I was his little sister so, of course, he wouldn't think I was very cool, and I wasn't old enough to hang out with him. He started to get into some trouble around town and his anger started to get the best of him. My mom decided to send him to a private school in Alberta. She felt he needed to get out of our small town and away from any bad influences. She believed it would be a positive opportunity for him. He attended a school in Stony Plain, Alberta, 10 hours away from us for his grade ten/eleven year and came back to our town for his grade twelve year. In hindsight, I don't believe the private school was a very positive experience. I do know he was beat there, which wasn't unusual in those days. The kids were often given the "strap" or the "paddle."

After graduating, he moved to Saskatoon. He was able to land himself a position at Air Canada. I thought he was finally on his way to happier, more fulfilling opportunities in the big city.

Sheldon was never one to talk on the phone or chat about inner feelings, so it was hard to know what was going on inside him. At times, he wouldn't return phone calls. You just had to keep calling him until you reached him. On one occasion, I visited him in Saskatoon. As I was leaving, he gave me his most prized possession, his stereo! I was surprised and said, "No, I can't take this!" However, he insisted I take it. With his good job, I figured he must have been buying himself a new stereo!

A few weeks later, he came to visit my mom and me in Regina. During one of our conversations, he made some unusual remarks. Later on, I asked my mom if she thought he could be contemplating suicide. She said, "yes" and that she had been trying to get him to go for help. She made many phone calls to social workers but was told to just "keep him talking. There is nothing you can do, unless he says he will harm himself or someone else." He never actually said those words, but some things he did say made me question his thoughts. The next morning, he took his life. I realize now that he gave me his most prized possession as a gift. He had come to visit mom and me to say goodbye. He never left a note. He was just gone. He was my only sibling, and I miss him dearly. Mental illness had taken my father and now, my only sibling.

My mother's childhood was filled with chaos. Her mother had an untreated mental illness, which made her moods unpredictable. My Grandpa and the children learned to walk on eggshells and stay outside on the farm, when possible. My mom left home at the age of sixteen.

My mother has had several nervous breakdowns in her adult life. She was eventually diagnosed with schizophrenia. Schizophrenia medication is a difficult medication as the side effects can deaden emotions and feelings. The patient doesn't always like how they feel while on the medication and therefore, many try to "control" their illness without medication. Or they feel really good on medication and believe they do not need it. Of course, this leads to the mental illness symptoms showing up. For my mother, this is fear and paranoia. When my mother chooses not to be medicated, she is very defensive and paranoid towards me. She doesn't tell me when she has gone off her medication so I am not aware. Other times she has told me she is on the medication, but she really isn't. Most of our adult relationship has been strained. Her irrational thinking causes many issues between us. Her brain tends to focus on negative thoughts that prove I do not care about her. Even though I try to explain my actions or the scenario, my explanations fall on deaf ears. You cannot change her mind about what she sees or thinks. For many years, I thought I was not a very good daughter and kept trying to "fix' myself and our relationship. We have been too many therapists to try to help us through our difficult times. However, in hindsight, her mental illness was never disclosed to any of these therapists. How could the therapist help us, if he didn't know what he was dealing with?

My mother and I both want a close relationship, so we keep working at it, but I realize and accept that it will likely never be the ideal mother/daughter relationship. She is not someone that I am able to turn to for support or someone I can go to for advice. With her mental illness, it is enough for her to keep herself well. I accept our relationship as it is and realize it is the mental illness that causes the problems and not my mother. (But it took me forty years to realize that!)

Thankfully, my mother is well enough to work, look after herself and enjoy her life. She has a big heart and lots of empathy for others going through hard times.

I have been diagnosed with anxiety/depression. When I am not on medication, the anxiety can get so bad that I do not even want to go to the grocery store. I do not want to see people or "pretend" I am ok. Inside my body, I can hardly breathe. It is a terrible strangling feeling. At times, I feel very sad and very lonely. I am not able to reach out to others for help because I honestly feel I have no friends, and I do not want to "bother" anyone. When I am experiencing this, the feelings and thoughts are very real, even though irrational. When taking medication, it's hard to believe I was thinking that way.

I went through one particular bad spell when I truly believed my husband and kids would be better off without me. I felt like a terrible person. I just wanted to lay in bed and sleep. I didn't want them to have to worry about me. It was the closest I have ever come to realizing what my brother had likely felt. I knew suicide was not an option because of what my mother and I had experienced with my brother. I am thankful I made it through that very dark time. I am thankful for my life. I believe it gives me empathy and understanding for those that suffer with mental illness. I have been blessed that my mental illness has been manageable for most of my life. I do feel blessed to enjoy my life and be able to live a mostly healthy happy lifestyle.

I do have three healthy adult children. They are all successful in their careers and personal lives. I am very close to them. At this time, none of them have been diagnosed with a mental illness. Is the cycle broken or is it waiting in the wings to strike at any time? Is mental illness inherited or is it a result of life circumstances and choices? In my opinion, it is all of the above. It is unpredictable and can show up at any time.

Mental illness affects all walks of life and all ages. There is no gender, income or race barrier. If you do not have a mental illness, I guarantee you know someone who does. Let's all just be a little more accepting and kind to one another!

Wendy Kimber

Hidden Secrets Hurt

MY NAME IS Sara Littlechief. When I was asked to write my story about my life with addictions to sobriety, it didn't take me long to reflect. My memories are right there when I look back at my past.

I'm a residential school survivor, taken away from my parents at a young age. I grew up in fear, anger, loneliness, violence and alcoholism. The loneliness I felt for my parents is indescribable, especially the loneliness for my mother. My parents both died from alcoholism, which I believe was caused by their built-up guilt, sadness and broken hearts because they were helpless at getting my sister and me back.

As time went on, my life went from bad to worse. I had secrets I thought I would hide from the light of day. Later finding out those secrets covered my peace and happiness. I was a little girl when I experienced mental, emotional, physical and sexual abuse. A sad and lonely life I lived, a life of fear. A life no child should ever live. No parents to turn to for comfort and protection. At night, I would cry silently to myself because crying was wrong and I could be punished. I wondered where my parents were, why I wasn't with them. I knew my little sister was in the building, but we had no contact. Life with my parents was not the best, but much better than this. At least with my parents, I was loved and comforted.

I got older and I went from residential school to foster homes, and I accepted that my parents were no longer part of my life. I remember my first suicide attempt; I was home for a visit at my grandparents. I couldn't handle the sadness and loneliness; that was the first time I didn't want to live; I took a knife and cut my wrist. My Googoo (my grandmother) used a traditional remedy to stop the bleeding because she couldn't get me to a doctor. She talked to me in tears as she was fixing my wrist, trying to scare me from trying it again by telling me that I would not go to a good place if I took my own life. If only I could tell her what was happening to me and how I missed my mom and dad, but I kept silent. Not long I was back in residential school or foster home. Can't remember, but I know I was taken away again.

At a young age, I was introduced to sniffing nail polish

remover to get high. I never went on such wonderful trips that took me away from my reality. But that only lasted for a while then the trips became my nightmares. After that I started drinking alcohol, that was much better; I had fun; I had courage. It was exciting, but I didn't know that this was going to be the beginning of almost ending my life.

I was put in my last foster home, which I ran from and that was the end of foster homes. I was fifteen years old and pregnant. I didn't drink alcohol or do drugs when I was pregnant. I became a mother when I was sixteen. I had my son; the baby I didn't want and the son who saved my life. I wrote at the beginning of my story a child should not live the life I lived, well, the majority of my cute, little son's life was dysfunctional because of my anger and addictions.

As time went on, I lost family and friends to suicide. The most devastating was when my mom died. My worst nightmare had come true; I couldn't imagine life without my mom, now she was gone. My alcoholism got worse. I went into blackouts every time I got drunk. Because of the awful things I was doing under the influence, I lost total respect from family and friends. As the years went on, terrible things happened to me. I was even more mentally and emotionally traumatized. I was physically and sexually assaulted more than once. I understand the fear of not speaking out on sexual assault, the fear of being judged and hated even more. One sexual assault I believe today, if I hadn't escaped, I would have been one of the missing and murdered women. When I escaped, out of terror, I stayed in a graveyard at night.

My life was a mess. I was leaving my son for days, even weeks, out on a binge. I had no idea if my son was safe or not, that was something I didn't think about. When I was drunk, I continued to hurt my family, friends and even people I didn't know. I had DUIs. I had a hit and run, I could have killed that family. I was so filled with fear, shame and guilt that I wanted to die. I tried suicide many times. Once, after another DUI, I knew I was going to jail. I didn't want to go to jail. I went home and took an almost full bottle of Valium only to wake up a few days later in my bed. I couldn't even do that right. A friend, my foster sister, talked to the judge, and I was sent to St. Louie Rehab for drunk drivers. This is where I first heard the words alcoholism and addiction. I also learned what denial is because that is what I did when I answered the twenty-one questions. I denied having an alcohol problem. I came home, abstained for about seven months, but in the mean time, I got addicted to more prescription pills, diet pills, Valium, sleeping pills, and painkillers. I needed pills to get me going in the morning. I needed pills to make me feel good. I needed pills for the bad headaches. I needed pills to help me sleep. I didn't think I could survive without the pills. I eventually went back drinking and doing drugs. My life was at its worst. I was twenty-six years old and my life was almost at an end. I got drunk and the cycle started again. I woke up sick, sorry, feeling guilty and ashamed. I was afraid. That morning, I lay in bed holding a pillow crying; crying so hard I couldn't breathe. I had no hope left, there was no way out but death. I heard my grandmother words about going to a place that was not good if I took my life. My thoughts were die and go to hell or live and live in hell. What a choice I had. Then I thought, "What if I just die and lie under the ground and not feel anymore." The thought of not feeling anymore made me excited. I jumped out of bed excited to die. I was at my kitchen ready to carry out my plan when suddenly, my son comes into the room, walks right in front of me and says, "Mom I'm coming for my shorts. I'm going swimming." He walked in and out. He had no idea what I was going to do. That's when I heard a voice say, "What's he going to do after you're gone? You know how it feels without a mom." I made a different plan. I'll go to work and do it after work. In the mean time, I'll write a letter to my sister to raise my son. While I was at work, I was so hung-over my hands and body were shaking as I tried to do my job. Suddenly, I heard the same voice saying, "call Andy, call Andy." Andy was the addiction worker who my grandmother always sent to help with no success. Out of fear, I called Andy. I told him if I went home I was going to die. He met me at my house. I broke down and told him what I was going to do and how hopeless I felt. Andy knew all about my addicted life because he lived in my community. Andy suggested I go to treatment. I didn't want to go, but then out of the blue, I made up my mind. I told him, "Ok I'll go." I went to the Estevan Treatment Centre on September 16, 1984. That was the last day I took my pills, which I took on the sly as Andy drove me to treatment. I have been sober and drug free since. To this day, I believe the voice I heard was my guardian angel. I wasn't going crazy because the voice guided me to change my life.

My first year of sobriety was the best. I used the coping skills from the treatment center. But my pent up anger, fear, low self-esteem and distrust started to surface and would make life unbearable to live again. I could not turn to alcohol or drugs to cover my feelings. My problems that I thought were caused from my addictions had continued to exist after I abstained.

I was now sober and miserable. I couldn't live like this, so I reached out to God. I called ministers, preachers, and AA members, but nobody was home. I was going to give up but decided to call one last church. A lady answered. I believe today God guided me to her because it was through her I met sister Denise. Sister Denise introduced me to inner child therapy. I did a lot of crying and anger work, then she told me about forgiveness. She told me that one day I would forgive the people that hurt me. That was not something I thought I would ever do, but it did happen. The hurt I caused people bothered me more than what happened to me. Those people didn't deserve what I did. My son didn't deserve the life he lived. Step nine in the AA Program "make amends to such people except when to do so would injure them or others" helped me with making amends. My healing journey began at three years sobriety.

I met another counselor who asked me, "Why are you dealing with the pain from here and going backwards when you should start from the beginning, dealing with those two people who were supposed to love and protect you, your parents, then come forward." The trauma in my life had to be dealt with. Thus, those deep dark secrets had to come out into the open for me to be at peace and happy. I started with the letter to my dad. Everything I needed to tell my dad I wrote down, pages and pages of anger. I was told, own your feelings, don't write you made me, instead write; I felt like this when you... did or said this. I had to take my power back. My dad did read my letter, and he confronted me with love. He said, "I didn't know you remembered all those things." Then he said, "I'm sorry, I love you." The wall fell down between us. An experience I will never forget. On his deathbed, my dad told me over and over he loved me. If I hadn't wrote the letter and forgave my dad and asked his forgiveness, I wouldn't have been by his side when he died. I would still be full of anger towards him. I also wrote a letter to my mother, the hardest letter to write because I loved my mom so much and did not want to see her with any faults. But yes, there was much more pain my mom caused because she was my role model to be a woman. She lived a life of alcoholism, abuse. Her anger came out when she was drunk. I cried and cried as I wrote her letter. The truth about how I really felt about my mom came out. I was angry. Why didn't she come get me and take me with her? She could have taken me away and hidden me. I wouldn't have cared how we lived, as long as I was with her. All my anger towards her came out. At the end of the letter like in my dad's, I told her I forgave her and asked her to forgive me for anything I did to hurt her. I had the most beautiful spiritual experience. I set my mom free; I set my dad free; I was free. I felt it was what they wanted me to do so I can live the life I always wanted: a sober and drug free happy life. The rest of the trauma and abuses were easier to deal with and let go.

I was finally convinced my alcoholism and drug addiction was not the root cause of my continuous anger, fear and loneliness. It was the trauma in my life and those deep, dark, hidden secrets that had to see the light of day.

I am thirty-two years sober drug free. The best decision I ever made was to go to treatment Sept 16, 1984. I am now a Certified Addiction Counselor and have worked in the addictions field for twenty-seven years. I understand alcoholism, drug and prescription drug addiction. I have empathy and compassion for addicts and those who are abused mentally, emotionally, physically and sexually. I am currently battling an incurable bone marrow disease. Every day is a gift. I am proud of my son and daughter who are both sober drug free. I am a grandmother and great grandmother. I have the man of my dreams. I met and made many wonderful friends in my sobriety. I am blessed.

My goal is to get my Addictions Specialist Diploma, which I am working on at the moment. I would also like to be a speaker to use my experience to give strength and hope to people who are struggling with addictions and life. I continue to go to AA meetings to help the new comers. I get one-on-one counseling when needed. I go to traditional ceremonies, and I also attend church.

"Then you will know the truth, and the truth will set you free." John 8:32

Sara Littlechief

Conal's Battle

CONAL WAS BORN MARCH 6, 1996 in Canmore Alberta, on a beautiful winter day. There was a fresh coat of snow on the ground, the mountains looked crisp, and the sky was clear and blue. You could see all the way down the valley. With so much love and anticipation, this beautiful child came into the world, into an incredibly large tight-knit family. He was our first child, and his grandparent's first grandson.

Nothing was more important to Conal than the love of his family. At the age of two, he became a big brother to his sister Macara. Instead of being jealous like many toddlers, he told everyone that she was his baby. He loved her and looked out for her as though she was his baby. For a long time, the two of them would take naps together while he held her little hand. They would play for hours without fighting.

At the age of four, Conal's little brother, Koa, was born.

For as long as we can remember, the boys have been inseparable. His extended family of cousins, aunties and uncles are a tight family unit and were a day-to-day part of Conal's upbringing. His cousins felt more like brothers and sisters to him as they grew up in each other's homes. There are eighteen altogether. The memories and qualities we cherish most about Conal have a recurring theme; his huge heart, his love for animals, nature, and for his family. He also had a silly laugh and the ability to bring that out in everyone around him.

Conal's love for animals was extraordinary. He would voraciously pursue any books he could find about almost any kind of animal. At four years old, he knew the difference between herbivores, carnivores and omnivores. Destined to be our biologist or zoologist. We were so proud! He could name specific species of reptiles, amphibians, equines, felines, canines and primates. He talked about how lions, tigers and leopards had retractable claws while the cheetah did not. He loved learning all these details. When he started kindergarten, he looked for the microscope in the classroom and was disappointed he couldn't find one.

His incredible sense of empathy allowed him to emulate these creatures that he loved to learn about. From the age of five, Conal went through a period of time where he would emulate a new creature every week. One week he was a cougar, the next a jaguar.

Conal showed us to appreciate some of the less desirable creatures of nature, like spiders, worms and through his absolute intolerance to the abuse of any living creature. He would frequently enlist his parents help to rescue a creature in need. Everything from grasshoppers being squished by neighborhood kids to removing the hundreds of frogs in the grass before mowing it.

Conal was an exceptional athlete. He played and excelled at baseball, basketball and football, but ultimately enjoyed challenging himself more than competing with others. He started martial arts at five years old, even though you normally had to be eight years old. He showed so much discipline and promise he was allowed to start early. Just three weeks after his sixth birthday, he broke a board with his forearm to earn his green belt in Krav Maga. He later moved onto study Hapkido, where he won countless gold medals in sparing and forms. He understood and loved the art of fighting.

Conal would frequently enlist his brother Koa, and cousins Zakk and Nash, to help him train in his various interests. He even studied swords for a time. The boys have fond memories of practicing swords with Conal, using the light saber swords his dad constructed for them out of golf tubes and electrical tape. When it came time to practice boxing, instead of the traditional protective gloves, Conal got them to cover their hands with pop boxes to practice. Conal was really strong, and being the oldest, was also the biggest in size, so after any wrestling match, sword beating session or boxing bout, Conal always took a moment to say " I love you man". He was a super loving guy and was never too cool to tell those around him that he loved them.

Conal was a natural leader, whether at school, in sports or amongst his cousins, his peers looked to him for guidance. He was one they knew they could count on. Conal held no prejudice, unless it was for witnessing unkindness. Of course it's hard to really understand the essence of a person through words. Let's put it this way, he would light up the room with his voice, his laugh, his warmth and his wit.

Conal's life was a message. He wanted us to remember what is important about life. He showed us compassion through his love for family, friends, and all living creatures. He didn't have time for pretense and popularity contests, and he didn't tolerate bullies. He appreciated simplicity, quietness, the importance of just "being" and really wanted the world to be a more loving place.

It was in Conal's grade eight year, that I started to notice him having days when he would seem more quiet, withdrawn, and lacking in energy and motivation. These days became more regular, despite having an incredibly wonderful last year in elementary. Even his teacher noticed this and mentioned it later in the school year. She said "you have a wonderful boy, but I have to tell you, that there are days when he seems to be carrying the weight of the world on his shoulders when he walks into class." His Hapkido instructor said the same thing not long after. I began noticing Conal finding it more difficult to get himself off to school. His absenteeism started to show a pattern. In the summer following, I saw him withdraw from his incredible friendships. He would start grade nine without these connections. I am pretty his past friends still wonder what they ever did wrong.

In grade nine, he started skipping school early in the year, alone mostly, to come home and go to bed. He was playing football at this time and although he claimed to love it, I would come home from work only to find out most days he didn't make it to school or practice. He had failing grades at his first report. I could not get him to open up about what was going on, so I decided to take him to see a social worker who came highly recommended by a friend. I took him there every two weeks for a couple months and under the advice of my family doctor put him on an antidepressant. The social worker told me that I have a healthy young man on my hands who is just really introverted and that things would work themselves out. Around this time, Conal was adamant he did not want to take antidepressants, so we allowed him to stop, not really knowing what the right decision was, but he was never given a diagnosis.

The next few years we would spend in a perpetual battle of starting and quitting school. We tried home schooling, online learning, three different high schools and an adult campus in Regina. In between these times, he held down jobs such as minor carpentry work and landscaping. He did seem to show more zest for life when he was working. We thought Conal would figure his life out and eventually go back to school, however, Conal often would mention to me that he felt lonely for friendships, despite being so close to his immediate and extended family. Being out of school at such a young age, connecting to peers was challenging and he eventually lost confidence. I also noticed he did not consistently care about his appearance.

Just before his eighteenth birthday, he decided to move with his dad in remote British Columbia, close to Nelson, where he would pursue his dream of living a life as an outdoorsman, surrounding by rich scenery and nature. He received a certificate for forest fire fighting and started forming some new friendships. I hadn't seen him happier in a very long time. Things were looking up that whole summer and into the fall. When the forest fire season had ended in October, his dad noticed he seemed to be quite down and encouraged him to come back to Regina because he thought Conal was just missing all of us. When he came back to Regina he decided to give school another shot at an adult campus, but this was short lived. I remember him saying "I just hate school mom!" I told him that I just wanted him to be happy and that if it meant not going to school, that I would support him. He decided he would wait for the fire season to start and go back to B.C. to work. I encouraged him to take some of the winter courses so that he would have work year-round. He agreed it was a good idea.

That winter and spring, Conal obviously fell into what was clearly a depression and would have late nights, followed by sleeping all day. He would often have late night drives alone and fill his days by not doing much else but watching movies. He was not eating much at all and appeared dishevelled, very flat affect. He developed somatic complaints such as chronic back pain that no one could find a cause for, yet it seemed so real to him.

In June, 2015, when I was talking about jobs and career opportunities to him, he told me that "there isn't really anything I am interested in anymore mom!" I will never forget how haunting those words were. Then he went on to tell me that he believed he was "losing his will." It was like the words were so hurtful that I could not comprehend them. I actually do not recall how I handled all of this and then he explained so matter of fact that he was spending his life pulling himself out of a dark hole of despair and he was growing tired. Just when he'd develop goals and got ready to pursue, he said it is like he falls off the edge of a cliff, suddenly, and rapidly, not in small increments. Then he started to cry, asking me "Why was it like this?"

I remember one late night; I abruptly woke up to the door closing. Out of concern, I got up to look for him and found him sitting on the roof of the house. I had never seen him look lower, flatter and more like someone beyond sad, like someone in trouble. I would take the next day off work, thinking I am going to get to the bottom of what was going on with him. The next morning I shouted downstairs to where he was sleeping and said "Come on, I am taking you for coffee." There was no response. I remember finding him lying on the floor where he would often stretch and work out. He was just laying there, his depression immobilizing him. I said "Son, what can I do for you, my sweet boy?" He looked up at me with helplessness and shook his head, "I don't know." I asked him if I could call my friend's husband who was a chaplain to come over. Conal nodded yes. The chaplain and Conal spent the whole day together. Conal divulged that he had had a plan to end his life, but that he could not allow himself to follow through because of not wanting to hurt his family. Together, the two of them went to the emergency room in Regina, to have Conal assessed. He was not admitted based on Conal agreeing to keep himself safe. There was no follow-up appointment made for Conal, no reconsideration of medication. He was asked to do some check-in phone calls to something like mobile crisis. Conal seemed to have a spring in his step after this day and quickly made plans to go back to B.C.

In B.C. that summer, he traveled with his dad, got a job serving at a pub, and fell in love with a girl. After breaking up with his girlfriend, he fell into a depression again. This was now the fall of 2015. I was checking on him regularly, worried about him because he had not wanted the relationship to end. On November 4th, 2015, Conal's dad phoned me to say that they couldn't find Conal, that he hadn't shown up for work and that the police were looking for him. Conal would later tell me that he was planning to end his life that day, but couldn't go through with it. The police insisted that he go to the local hospital. Conal went willingly. This would be his first and only hospitalization. He had been drinking alone which had become somewhat of a pattern. The two weeks he spent in the hospital, he had resigned himself to trying medication and was really reaching out for help. The health care staff said he was a ray of sunshine and really seemed to have no doubt he would be ok.

He flew back to Regina November 21st with my suggestion, so I could help him adjust to his medication and give him some close emotional support. We had five magical weeks with Conal, who seemed so invested in a future. He was going to stay in Regina and finish his high school. He had made his own follow-up appointment with a psychiatrist in order to have his medication and progress monitored. He was feeling pretty good on the medication. He was becoming socially engaged again, phoning up some of his old friends, going clothes shopping, helping out around the house, helping look after his little sister, going to his brother's and cousins sporting events. He even planned on making music with his little brother, with new equipment they got for Christmas. He was even doing Yoga and trying to get me to join with him.. He was confiding in me lots which made me believe he would each out if he became low again. He shared with me, during this time in B.C., the low he experienced prior to his hospitalization in was "terrifying," something he never wanted to experience again, but agreed he would reach out for help if it did.

On December 23rd, he told his grandma and me that he was starting to feel low again, and how he was "so sick of this". I broke out a board game (Kronono) to try to lighten the mood. It seemed to work. I got very busy with the last minutes things for Christmas, and Conal seemed okay, excited about the cookies I was baking. He even took his little sister to have a pic taken with Santa. I remember having to peel him away from making music Christmas day to go to his Auntie's for supper. He left early that night, saying he had to go make music, but now I have my doubts it was just that. On Boxing day, he was excitedly planning to go shopping for me and to pick out paint so we could paint the house together, but he never made it out. He spent the day in bed, stating he was sick from all the junk food he ate. I left for a night shift at around seven at night, giving Conal and my other children a casual goodbye, never anticipating it would be the last time I would see my son alive. In the early hours of December 27th, at the age of nineteen, Conal ended his own life, bringing to a close, his five year battle with depression. Such a young life lost. Through the grief of losing him, I believe I have been given a glimpse of his heartache and this will fuel me to work for more understanding and supports to those living with mental illness.

Vanessa Vogel

Goodbye Paycheck

LIFE TRULY IS AN INTERESTING THING! One day you think you have everything figured out and then suddenly, BOOM, you get completely derailed!

Hi, my name is Darren Neuberger and I was born and raised in Weyburn, Saskatchewan. My parents are Bernie & Ella Neuberger and I have three older brothers, Tim, Dan, Todd and a younger sister Michelle, or as I often call her, that girl who ruined our chances of having an all Neuberger boy infield! Life in Weyburn was great! I played a lot of sports, well, let's just say that was my life and I made a lot friends, many of who are still best buds to this day!

Fast forward to the year 2000, the new millennium! This was geared up to be a life changing, exciting year for me because I was getting married and my fiancé (now my wife) were starting a brand new chapter in our lives, in a brand new province and a brand new city! What I wasn't expecting was that I was also going to have a gambling addiction! What was supposed to be the best year of my life quickly turned into a hollow, physically and mentally draining existence! Slot machines, which they didn't have in Weyburn, took over my entire being! The lure of that "BIG WIN" mesmerized me! I became possessed and it was nothing to spend an entire paycheck in one sitting because the next pull on that big handle will be the one! The funny thing is that it wasn't, nor was the next one or the next one and before you know it, my paycheck was gone in about fifteen minutes! One would think that you would stop, but not me. Maybe it's the competitive nature that I have instilled in me from a very early age or perhaps it was compulsive disorder that I also have had from an early age, probably both! The loss of money and the thrill of the big win had me, and it was all that I could think about, all the while unbeknownst to me, it was killing me inside!

All "good things" eventually will come to an end and my end was when my wife and mom figured out that something was wrong! I felt like I was being interrogated by my wife and finally I cracked and confessed that I had been gambling, a lot and it was then that I was given the ultimatum to seek help or our marriage was over. I sought help and found a Gamblers Anonymous meeting and this is where my road to recovery starts!

Attending GA was a huge hit to my ego and, although I didn't feel I had an addiction, I quickly learned that I did and boy that was a gut check! I was abstinent from gambling for over a year and one day while driving I thought I was cured, stopped in the casino and lost two hundred dollars in five minutes and quickly got the hell out of there, called my sponsor in tears and October 11, 2001 was the last time I ever placed a bet! I'm going to be brutally honest with you, the aftermath of an addiction, for me anyways, was horrible! I was practicing the 12 Step Program, which is based on the one made famous by AA, and having to relive what I went through, make amends to the people I lied to, come face to face with the reality that I was a "loser" (my own self thoughts) was a tough pill for me to swallow! I appeared to be the same old happy, fun loving Red that everybody knows and loves on the outside, but when I went home with my thoughts at the end of the day I hated myself, I was dying inside and I couldn't even look at myself in the mirror because I hated the person that was looking back at me! As a matter of fact, for the better part of a year, I would say one simple prayer each night before I went to sleep. "God, it would be okay if I didn't wake up in the morning!" Fast forward to December2, 2002, one day before my thirty-fourth birthday and I woke up with a clarity that I have never felt before and that was, this is the day I'm going to end my life! For the better part of three hours, I sat with a bottle in my hand and I would put them in my mouth, then I would take them out and I would do that about fifteen times before I finally stood up and threw those pills across the hardwood floor in the one bedroom duplex that my wife and I were renting! As I watched those pills bounce I saw those pills as a reflection of all of the pain, hurt and suffering I had caused to the people who I loved the most and in the other pills I saw the good that I have done and given to others. I saw the people who loved me the most and thought of the pain I would have forever left them with, had I gone ahead and taken my life. That was enough for me to quickly pick those pills up and flush them down the toilet!

I remember dropping down to my knees and screaming in tears "God, what do you want from me?" What I have learned from the depression, anxiety, angst and pain of living with an addiction is that I'm not weak. I had an illness and I'm grateful for the help that I sought after and by not living in silence with this addiction is what truly saved my life. If you are suffering, then seek help because your loved ones would rather have a "damaged you" as opposed to not having you at all.

Eight months after the suicide attempt, I was diagnosed

with acute lymphoblastic leukemia and my prayer to God quickly changed to "God, please let me live!" I was thirty-four years old and in the fight for my life! My cancer story is long, so I will just share a quick version. I was officially diagnosed with cancer on August 1, 2003. On August 5th I was admitted as an inpatient to the Tom Baker Cancer Centre at the Foothills Hospital in Calgary and started chemotherapy on August 6 (no rest for the wicked)! I was in treatments for two years straight. As an inpatient for the first five months, I had over six hundred chemo treatments, two weeks of brain radiation, and one trip to the intensive care unit due to ecoli. I never should have survived because I had a fever of 106.5 and my blood pressure dropped to 52/32 and the reason for it was I had no immune system to fight it off. But after having over thirty-four blood and platelet transfusions, I'm still here today! Near the end of my two years in treatments I started having anxiety, depression and survivor guilt. My wife encouraged me to seek help, again, and I did! It was the best thing that I ever did and because of that, to this day, I help and mentor thousands of cancer patients from all parts of the world so they to can live their lives to the fullest, in a new way, and never look back!

The derailment that I mentioned at the start of my story is something that you can never predict. For the most part it, is truly out of your hands, but the message that I want you take away from this is to never think that you have to go through something alone! Asking for help is not a sign of weakness. It necessary! We all face our inner demons and go through many challenges, but trust me, the moment you let go of your ego and accept the fact that you're only human and that there are so many people who would do anything to help you, support you, and love you is the exact moment that you will be able to heal! I will leave you with a quote and please read this as many time as you have to when you are feeling like you can't go on because trust me, you can!

"You are always BIGGER than IT, no matter WHAT your IT IS!"

Darren Neuberger

Tears & Mascara

"Sexual assault is the only violent crime in Canada that is not declining." - canadianwomen.org

BEING MY FATHER'S only daughter, he lived with a lot of fear that anything 'bad' could happen to me. When I was just in preschool, he warned me to be cautious of strangers and taught me how to phone home. When I was seven, he put me in Taekwondo and always asked questions to make sure I felt safe at a sleepover. At twelve, he trained me in self-defence and taught me how to escape from an assailant. At thirteen, he talked to me about how to avoid at risk situations, and how to say no if feeling pressured by a boy. At fourteen, he told me not to get rides from the older boys, even if it happened to be my friend's big brother. When I was fifteen, I enrolled in Brazilian kickboxing on my own. By sixteen, I was at my physical peak. I was strong, smart, capable and careful.

A few months before my seventeenth birthday, I attended a small party with several kids from school. At this party, I was unknowingly given a paralytic drug. I started to feel dizzy and nauseous. I remember staring into the sink as the faucet dripped and feeling a numb sensation spread over my entire body. The guy I had come with encouraged me to get some fresh air outside. He suggested that perhaps the smoke was getting to me. I wandered onto the lawn and vomited as my legs began to shake. He came behind and kindly guided me to the passenger seat of my car. My tongue felt heavy in my mouth, my muscles weak and limp. My mind, however, was racing and alert. I was conscious when I was raped. And no amount of self-defence could have prevented it from happening.

It's harder to talk about the second time I was raped. I think it's because at one point I loved my rapist. He had been a decent boyfriend, a little jealous, a little controlling, but otherwise, he was just that: a typical, high school boyfriend.

So when he saw me years after we broke up, stumbling into the parking lot of my favourite nightclub after a night of dancing and laughter with my closest friends, I didn't expect him to look at me and see an opportunity. But he did. Unfortunately, my best friend was still inside, just a few minutes too late.

It happened so quickly. I remember seeing his face and thinking it was funny he was standing there watching me. He took a few long strides from his car and was trying to grab my sleeve, but I didn't want him to touch me. Next thing I knew, I was on the ground of the parking lot, and I was screaming. I was begging for the bouncer to save me. I was just wearing a dress as my knees and my face hit the pavement. He dragged me by my arms across the parking lot.

Tears and mascara streamed down my face as I screamed out yelling, "stop, save me, don't let him take me." The last thing I saw was the bouncer laughing and shaking his head.

Cut to the next day... I woke up in a bed I didn't recognize, bandages on my knees and elbows. Blood dried to my skin. I was so sore like someone had cut me open inside. I hadn't felt like this the first time I was raped because the first time I couldn't resist. This time my battle had left me wounded, and everything that happened was coming into my mind as fragments—strange, shattered images that I couldn't piece together.

My best friend walked into the room with a cup of water for me. I readjusted a little and looked around his room because that's where I was: on his king-sized bed with bandages and blood on his nice, white sheets. Tears sprung to my eyes. Maybe I didn't understand something? Maybe last night hadn't been as horrific as these flashes in my mind?

"What happened to me, why do I feel like this... did we? We didn't have sex, did we Scotty?"

Tears sprung to his eyes, as he quietly shook his head no.

"Did somebody do this to me... Who did this? Why?" So many questions tumbled out of my mouth as my stomach churned.

"I am so sorry Kealy, I'm gonna take you home, and you need to rest. I'll explain everything later I promise."

A few hours later after he had dropped me off, there was a knock at the door. My best friend stood in front of me. He no longer had a look of sorrow but anger. He asked me to come outside. He grabbed my ex and put him in front of me.

"Tell her what happened; tell her what you did."

My ex looked at my feet, never raising his eyes. "I took you home..." he paused, and Scott nudged him hard. "And I had sex with you."

I took a few steps backward. I looked at my knees. I looked at Scott, and then he looked me in the eyes, and I said it.

"You raped me last night." I continued to back away. I walked in my duplex, and I puked on the floor.

I spent years unable to cope with what had happened to me. Keeping it bottled inside, scrubbing at my skin night after night. I would burst into tears spontaneously when I'd consider getting "close" with someone else. I eventually sought help, and thanks to a wonderful counsellor with Saskatoon's Mental Health and Addictions Services, I was able to access resources that led me to a place of healing and was diagnosed with Post Traumatic Stress Disorder. I attended the Women's Anger and Self-Esteem Group, which led me to releasing a lot of the emotions I'd buried for so long. On December 7th 2009, I took one of the most important steps to becoming the woman I am today. I chose to remove my crutches and live a life of sobriety. I am now a successful finance manager, a professional model with Infinity Modelling Agency, an aspiring actor and a passionate writer. Today, I am confident. I am proud, and I spend my time being an advocate for young men and women who've been through similar experiences.

Kealy Cheyenne

Anxiety Attacks

MY FATHER WAS DIAGNOSED WITH schizophrenia when I was a young child. I lived with his troubles with the law and his strange ideas about being careful not to talk too loud about various things when there was a radio going. He believed it could go through the radio waves where others could hear it. He also had delusions of grandeur, also common for schizophrenia.

He spent the last three years of his life in the Tatagwa View Long Term Care facility, and was blessed with very patient and caring staff. The only way to sum up Dad's personality was diverse and complex. Every day was different. Dealing with his mental illness, and all that accompanied it, certainly took us on some wild rides.

Mom had a lot of stress dealing with my dad's illness and alcoholism, and they divorced when I was seven years old. Oddly enough, it seems like most of her mental health problems came after the divorce. Perhaps that

148

wasn't the case, and it was just that she was finally able to relax, and let her guard down. I'm not sure. It also could have been that I didn't really notice anything until I was older. She was on medication for depression for as long as I can remember. She still is, and she will be turning seventy-seven this year. For the most part, she has done quite well on medication. I do recall a few incidences during my teenage years where she had to be admitted to a hospital of some sort for psychiatric treatment. All I remember is one time my stepdad took me for a visit, and for most of the visit mom cried. I found it quite upsetting.

In 1992, mom was diagnosed with breast cancer, and then again in 2004. She was like a warrior. She took her treatments, and carried on with an impressive strength. I don't know where it came from. She truly handled both cases with amazing grace and determination.

I am very grateful I didn't develop schizophrenia or clinical depression. I have, however, struggled with periods of anxiety and anxiety attacks. It started between the time I had my first and second child. I remember being home one afternoon, when suddenly this weird feeling came over me, and I felt like I couldn't breathe. I just wanted to get away. Those symptoms continued and grew stronger. One incident had gotten so terrible that the anxiety increased so bad while being in the grocery store and having to leave without paying for my groceries. Or going for a walk with my husband and son, and not getting far before I had to turn around and get home. I just felt so uncomfortable. This went on for some time before I finally went to my doctor and explained what I was experiencing. A referral to a specialist was made and I started to see a therapist who taught me different ways to think of things and how to use different coping methods. It was a great help and I will always be grateful to her for turning things around for me.

Today, people tell me I am so easygoing. I don't know if that is always the case. I am guilty of turning stress inward and have issues with stomach problems and tachycardia. I just try to be kind to myself and not get too bent out of shape over things that really aren't worth sacrificing my health for.

Everyone has a story. For the longest time, I kept mine to myself. It was embarrassing at the time. Would I be judged because of my parents? Would I be judged because of my anxiety? What I have discovered, and maybe that wisdom comes a bit with age, is that I think people appreciate honesty and realness. It's only by sharing my story, experiences, and knowledge, that I am able to help other people.

In closing, I want to mention three people. Grant (my grade twelve grad partner), Perry (a friend of my husband's family), and Spencer (my co-workers son). These three men took their lives by suicide. I hope this book will help to end any stigma around mental illness and people will be more comfortable in coming forward and asking for help.

Angie Neuberger

Resources
Books

"Switch on Your Brain" by Dr. Caroline Leaf
("Thoughts are real, physical things that occupy mental real estate. Moment by moment, every day, you are changing the structure of your brain through your thinking. When we hope, it is an activity of the mind that changes the structure of our brain in a positive and normal direction. We are not victims of our biology...")

"Stress, Anxiety, and Insomnia: What the Drug Companies Won't Tell You and Your Doctor Doesn't Know" by Michael T. Murray, N.D.
(Dr. Michael Murray provides insight into the many causes of unhealthy stress, and explains why the drug approach generally doesn't work. He gives practical advice and guidance on how to cope with stress naturally along with tips and strategies for all aspects of stress management, from managing time and relationships to healthy eating, exercise, and achieving a positive attitude.")

"Three Brains: How the Heart, Brain, and Gut Influence Mental Health and Identity" by Karen Jensen, N.D.
("The brain has been studied for centuries and amazing discoveries have been made. Research now suggests that you actually have three brains: the heart, the gut and the head brain. There is an intricate relationship

between these three brains that influences mental health and optimal brain function"...."There is growing evidence that nutrients from whole foods, exercise, and supplements are effective, non-invasive ways to help prevent and treat many mental health and neurological disorders associated with imbalances between the three brains.")

"Win the Battle: The 3-Step Lifesaving Formula to Conquer Depression and Bipolar Disorder" by Bob Olson; Chandler House Press; 1999

"The Noonday Demon: An Atlas of Depression" by Andrew Solomon; Scribner; 2001

Distress Lines

Prince Albert Mobile Crisis Unit
(306) 764-1011

Regina Mobile Crisis Services
(306) 525-5333

Saskatoon Mobile Crisis
(306) 933-6200

Mobile Crisis Help Line
(306) 757-0127

Crisis Text Line
741741

Counsel

Wheatland Community Church of Weyburn
46-12th Street
Phone: (306) 842-2429
Email: wheatlandcc@sasktel.net
www.wheatlandcommunitychurch.ca
(I am Ed Fischer, pastor of Wheatland Church. I have
worked with many people who have struggled with
addictions, and I personally am a recovered alcoholic,
so I understand. I am willing to share how I broke free
and give you other tools to get yourself on to the road
to recovery.)

Geri Holmes
(306) 471-8817
Estevan and Weyburn

Ron Lund at PAR Consultants
(306) 352-0680

Leigh Tomilin, BSW
Mental Health and Addictions Services
Community Health Services Building
Box 2003, Weyburn, SK, S4H 2Z9
Email:Leigh.Tomilin@schr.sk.ca
Tel: (306) 842-8693
Fax: (306) 842-8692

Narcotics Anonymous
Alcoholics Anonymous

24-hour service
(306) 842-2334

Kipling Addiction Services
(306) 736-2363

Estevan St. Joseph's Addiction Services
(306) 637-2422 or (306) 637-2465

Regina Detox
(306) 766-6622

Larson Detox
(306) 655-4195

Sask Health Line
811

Wakamow Manor
(306) 694-4030

Crisis Beds
http://www.mobilecrisis.ca/available-beds

Treatments

Transcranial Magnetic Stimulation (TMS) Therapy

TMS therapy is a neurophysiological technique to treat depression and anxiety. The magnetic coil that is used in the TMS therapy generates a magnetic field around the frontal lobe of the brain, which stimulates the area called Dorso Lateral Pre Frontal Cortex (DLPFC), which is the area involved in the regulation of mood, feelings and anxiety. The patient hears only a ticking noise during the treatment and the effect of the magnetic field in the brain is painless. TMS therapy has been used since 1984. The patient is fully alert during the treatment and can do meditation or practice a brief relaxation technique. Health Canada has approved it for the treatment of major depressive disorder and anxiety disorders.

The patient can be referred by their family doctor or specialist, and it is covered if you have a Saskatchewan Health Card.

Advantages of TMS Therapy: Painless procedure, non-invasive, no anesthesia required, outpatient therapy, effectiveness only requires 4-6 weeks of treatment, ability to provide therapeutic benefit for treatment-resistant individuals, patients do NOT have to stop taking medication in order to receive TMS therapy, non-responders typically achieve a 15 percent reduction in depression symptoms, equivalent effectiveness in treating both patients with Major Depressive Disorder and those suffering from Bipolar Disorder, treatment parameters are determined individually for each patient.

Potential side effects are mild to moderate headache, particularly in the first few sessions which responds well to Tylenol. Occurrence of seizures is an extremely rare possibility, and with the newer techniques it is almost unheard of.

There are clinics for TMS treatments in Regina and Saskatoon.

Acupuncture

Taka Iida

(306) 861-9545

MY COPING PLAN

☐ Call Distress Line at _____
(24 hour service) for emotional support

☐ Call the crisis team at _____
for emotional support and the possibility of
accessing the crisis beds

☐ Go to the emergency room _____
to be assessed by a physician

☐ Go to your doctor _____

☐ Call 911 for emergency support

☐ Call a friend/family member for emotional
support and/or to have them stay with you

☐ Engage in self-care activities for relaxation
and release, such as:

    o Listening to positive music

    o Exercise

    o Writing/drawing my thoughts in a
      journal

    o Access your higher power/spiritual
      guide

    o Breathe (i.e., in for a count of 3, hold
      for a count of 3, release for a count
      of 3 for 5 or more minutes)

    o Spend time in your safe/relaxing
      place real or imaginary

    o Tight/relax relaxation exercise (hold
      shoulders really tight for 5 seconds,
      then relax etc.)

    o Repeat your favourite mantra, or
      positive self-talk statement

○ **Other** _____

○ **Other** _____

☐ **Say: Feeling this way is temporary. Feelings change—with healthy action and self-talk**

*If I am having thoughts of wanting to hurt someone else,
I agree to access my resources above as alternatives:*

Signature: Date:

_____   _____

Dominic's

Dominic's place is an affordable housing, fourteen apartment complex with large common areas, located in Weyburn, SK and operated by the Weyburn Group Homes Society Inc. The tenants that reside in the complex are individuals, eighteen years of age and over, who have a diagnosis of serious enduring mental illness and/or addictions.

Staff, along with a team of other partnering professionals, provide support for the development of daily living skills, coping and problem solving skills, medication management, financial (budgeting) skills, and other life wellness skills. The focus of the program is to develop and maintain independent living skills and create an improved quality of life with a sense of belonging to a community. Dominic's program strives to provide tenants with confidence and skills to access resources to increase their capacity and skills to access resources to increase their capacity to be successful and feel satisfied within the living, working, and social environments of their choice.

Proceeds from the sales of this book will be donated to Dominic's.

THANK YOU

To our contributors:

Amber Istace	Jeff Heisler
Angela Tichkowsky	Kathy Gagne
Angie Neuberger	Kealy Cheyenne
Carol Borys	Mikayla Lohse
Chris Borshowa	Pamela Guest
Dawna Mellon	Paul Heebner
Darren Neuberger	Ramona Iida
Erin Francais	Sandy Johnson
Geoff Brown	Sara Littlechief
Greg Brown	Tanis Francis
Harmony Melnychuk	Vanessa Vogal
Janice Seitz	Wendy Kimber
Jeff Bartsch	

Darren Neuberger, Ramona Iida,
Geoff Brown, Colin Folk
for spearheading this project and being champions of
mental health awareness

Christopher Borshowa (owner of Phantasma Photography)
for the cover photo. www.phantasmaphotography.net

Publisher Richy Roy (Prestige Book Publishing)
for bringing the project to life
www.prestigepublishing.ca

Additional thanks to Phyllis O'Connor, Trudy Morken,
Theresa Girardin, Bernice Driscoll, Aspen Orsted, Kenton
Field, Kelley Wilson and the many people that helped
spread the word of the project.